Footprints of Five Generations

C.W. Schmidt

Edited by Stephen A. Engelking

Footprints of Five Generations

C.W. Schmidt
© 2021 Edited and with notes by
Stephen A. Engelking

Texianer Verlag, Tuningen, Germany
www.texianer.com

ISBN: 978-3-949197-83-3

Frontispiece

Good-by, old house, where happy children played;
Good-bye, old house, where hopes were born;
Good-bye, old house, where death took its toll;
You will soon cease to be even a milestone or a landmark.

Table of Contents

Frontispiece..3

Preface..7

A Man Without a Country...9

Foreword..11

How New Ulm Got It's Name..................................13

New Ulm in Its Infancy...17

The Immigrants...21

New Ulm Had an Interesting Beginning.............25

Pioneer Physicians of New Ulm..........................35

Pioneers Had Few Comforts of Life....................37

Reminiscences of a Native Austin Countian......43

Glimpses of Pioneer Life...47

How Industry Got Its Name....................................53

The School House..61

A Prairie Fire...65

Breaking Oxen..69

Entertainment...71

Hunting Game..73

Locating Bee Trees...75

Hogs Fatten on Mast..79

Going a Fishing..81

New Ulm, Texas, Older than New Ulm, Minnesota..85

Within the Covers of the Family Album............89

Cat Spring...95

New Bremen..97

Frelsburg..99

New Ulm A Railroad Town..............................107

The German Element......................................111

Beginnings of New Ulm, Minnesota.................115

Big Trees from Little Acorns Grow..................127

The Pathfinders..133

Editor's Introduction

This little but interesting book originally written in the 1930's is a mine of useful information for those interested in the pioneer beginnings of Texas. It has not been available for a long time and the extant copy which could be found was a facsimile in rather poor condition.

The whole book has now been transcribed and considerably edited. Additional notes have been added where appropriate.

I apologize for the poor condition of the photographs but I thought it better to include them for the sake of interest and completeness.

I hope you enjoy reading some of these first hand accounts as passed on by the author as I did.

Stephen A. Engelking, Editor

A Man Without a Country

"Youngster" Philip Noan said, "if you are ever tempted to say a word or to do a thing that shall put a bar between you and your family, your home, and your country, pray God in His mercy to take you that instant home to His own heaven. Stick by your family, boy; forget that you have yourself, while you do every thing for them. Think of your home, boy; write and send, and talk about it; Let it be nearer and dearer to your thought the farther you have to travel from it. And for your country, boy and for her flag, never dream a dream but of serving her as she bid you, though the service carry you through a thousand hells. No matter what happens to you, no matter what flatters you or who abuses you, never let a night pass but you pray God to bless that flag. Remember, boy, that behind all these men that you have to do with, behind officers and government, and people even, there is the Country, your Country, and that you belong to Her as you belong to your mother. Stand by her, boy, as you would stand by your mother."

Foreword

In compiling this modest little manual, the author aimed at originality and intelligibleness rather than transposing, recasting and reproducing reading matter contained in manuals of like import. The field covered by the present volume is not entirely unoccupied. For instance, the narrations of Herman Ehrenberg, Bernhard Monken, Ludolf F. Lafrentz, Adolf Stern, F. W. Luhn, Wilhelm Herms, Fritz Schlecht and others are carefully preserved and found on every library shelf in the homes where love and esteem for the pioneer exists. Then, too, about the year 1899, W. A. Trenckmann, editor of "Das Wochenblatt," then located at Bellville, published a booklet entitled "Austin County"[1], which has been read and reread until its leaves are worn to shreds, impairing its further usefulness. About the year 1914 the imminent writer and historian, Professor Duncan of Chicago, began the compilation of one of the most comprehensive treaties on pioneer life ever published. Duncan's publications consists of five large volumes and retailed at $30.00 per set, which accounts for the sale of fewer than one hundred copies in this County.

1 "A History of Austin County, Texas". Edited and published in 1899 as a supplement to the Bellville Wochenblatt by William A. Trenckmann Translated by his children William, Else, and Clara. Published in Texianer Verlag ISBN: 978-1511991605.

There are yet among us men and women who braved the dangers and hardships of a frontier life in order that we may be enjoying the advantages and wealth of the present. Some of these have not great wealth and while others are drawing a small pension from the State, there are still others who are in dire poverty and never expect to ride on a concrete highway for pleasure and recreation. What they want to know more than anything else is that their lives have not been spent in vain; that we are actually building on the foundation they have laid; and that we appreciate just what they have done.

Those were strenuous times when pioneer men and women had to be brave and face the dangers that threatened home and children; the men could not always be near to protect their families and their property; but seldom do we hear or read of a woman who did not nobly and bravely stand between her loved ones and danger, whether from dangerous wild animals, marauding redskins or from a devastating prairie fire that often swept the settlement, leaving nothing but a black streak of ashes in its wake. It is hard indeed for us to realize as we sit beside our peaceful firesides, the hardships and perils those brave men and women had to endure when this country was an untamed wilderness. Therefore, we dedicate this manual to their memory.

C.W. Schmidt

How New Ulm Got It's Name

In the death of J. C. Duff in the year 1850, the settlers lost one of their best friends and counselors. Dishonest characters, who had feared Duff now drifted into the peaceable settlement and started annoying the settlers and molesting their property. A mass meeting was called by the settlers to deliberate for the purpose of mutual protection and combining strength and intelligence to uphold law and order. The meeting was called to convene in the old town hotel, an old rambling log cabin structure, which was widely known for the splendid accommodations and service extended to the guests and for the hospitality that prevailed.

It was a gala day for the settlers and much excitement prevailed because of the long distance settlers had to travel over unfenced prairies and through dense timberland in order to reach their destination.

The hotel manager and his family had prepared an excellent dinner for the delegates of whom it was expected that they bring their families. It was to be a great convention of law abiding settlers, inasmuch as the time had now come to petition the government for the establishment of a post office; and, of course, the new town had to be christened with all possible pomp and ceremony. At noon, the improvised long table accommodating twenty-six diners, was set with the finest of victuals the country afforded. Just prior to the dining period, a stranger, who had terrorized and annoyed the settlers upon various previous occasions and who, without ever offering any pay or showing appreciation for letting him eat and sleep in the homes of the settlers, rode up to the hostelry, tied his gotch-eared mustang pony to a tree, went inside the hotel and made himself a home against the wish of the landlord. He was endowed with considerable nerve and was a rough looking subject. He was scantily and slovenly dressed. He rode a center fire or single cloth Yankee saddle and pretended to pose as a "two-gun man"—that is to say, he wore a heavy cap and ball six-shooter on either hip. The fact that the lower ends of his holsters were tied down, in order to facilitate the easy withdrawal of the pistols, seemed to indicate that he expected to use them. He had, furthermore, a quiet eye, with the glint of steel that bore out the inference of the tied holsters. Not waiting to be welcomed or for an invitation to eat at the table, he accosted the landlord to reserve two chairs for him at the dining table. He sat in one; the other he used as a place to deposit his hat. He had previously told the landlord that under no circumstances must he seat a guest in the second chair and warned him that he would kill any man who tried to occupy it. When all the guests were seated Lorenz Mueller, a six-footer, blue-eyed and brave as a lion, found no place at the table for him except in the chair in which the hat of the mysterious stranger reposed. Mueller was about to occupy it when the landlord rushed up and whispered that it meant certain death to use the chair. Lorenz Mueller however, who had some experience as a cow-puncher and trail driver, calmly took the hat, pitched it into the fire in the fireplace, barely missing a venison roast and sat down in the chair. The mysterious man was so amazed at the unexpected action of Lorenz Mueller that he left his meal unfinished, walked out of the hotel in a jiffy, disappeared in the forest and never returned to act a bully in the settlement thereafter.

After the diners had regained their composure and congratulated Lorenz Mueller for his daring deed, the meeting was called to order amidst a boisterous ripple of laughter and shouts of merriment, whereupon Mueller treated the delegates to some imported wine and other beverages. Lorenz Sailer, Mueller's brother-in-law, suggested that the post office be named New Ulm in honor of Ulm in Wuertemberg, Germany, from which country most of the settlers had come, which was approved by the delegates without opposition. Mueller, who owned a mercantile business was subsequently appointed first post master of New Ulm, Texas.

About the year 1858, Mueller sold his mercantile establishment to Ernst Wangemann, and removed to Llano County, where he became a large landowner and stock raiser. He owned the largest sheep ranch in the country adjacent to what was formerly Indian Territory, now Oklahoma, and later became interested in mining. The whereabouts of his descendants are not known.

During the pioneer days, banks were unknown. Consequently all purchase money was paid cash on the barrel end. Often several hundred dollars in silver was carried in saddle bags or in strong canvas sacks tied to the pommel of the saddle. There were no hijackers, bandits, yeggmen or robbers because there was no means of escape by which they could elude punishment at the hands of their victims.

On one occasion, a settler missed $300.00 in silver from his saddle bags. A vigorous search was immediately instituted but no trace of the money could be found. All joined in the search for the missing treasure save one newcomer who had not been there very long. On questioning him, he denied having taken the money. A day or two later, the accused was trying to leave the party, pretending that he had been innocently accused of stealing money. One of the party threw a rope about him with the avowed understanding that he choose the alternative of returning the stolen money or forfeit his life. He chose the former, giving detailed accounts of where he had hidden the money. His confession under duress caused a bruise that ointment could not heal. He swore vengeance but was never permitted to carry out his threat. He left one evening ostensibly to attend a house party in a neighboring village and that was the last the settlers ever heard of him. He died of lead poisoning, according co unconfirmed rumors.

New Ulm in Its Infancy

In 1852, when New Ulm was established a post office town, the people believed in the brotherhood of man, and lived a happy and contented life; perhaps, because of the restrictions forced upon them for lack of transportation facilities. They stood by one another in sickness and in health; laughed and wept together and willingly and cheerfully contributed their mite in lessening the burdens of the weak and sharing the protection of the strong. They inherited from their Christian parents the high ideals and the strength of character which were the priceless assets brought with them when they came to settle here and to undergo the hardships that are incident to pioneering a country.

Immediately upon their landing, they started building rude log houses with dirt floors. The settlers who had come with S. F. Austin's colony showed them how to build a frame, rolled huge logs upon it and sawed the logs with a whip saw and thus made planks for tables, benches, wagonbeds, coffins and so forth. One man stood on the top of the frame and the other under it and sawed up and down following the black lines made on the logs for direction. As the first settlers did not have glass windows on their arrival here, they had small openings cut out of the log walls, substituting wooden doors, fastened by hinges on the inside of the building for glass. When they wished to keep them open, they fastened them back to the walls with hooks.

The stores and business houses were built of logs. The proprietor and his family lived in one

Franz Pille—Pioneer of New Ulm, Texas

end of the log building and kept store in the other. In the pioneer days, merchants kept very small stocks of goods or merchandise, because of the distance freight had to be hauled and for lack of capital. The early freight transportation between New Ulm and Houston was carried on by ox-wagons. According to an estimate by old timers, there were three or four thousand ox-wagons engaged thus in Texas, and each wagon required from five to eight yoke oxen. Groceries and other merchandise were hauled away from

Houston to all parts of the state in these wagons. Some of them carried great loads of barrels containing whiskeys and vinegar. That the teamsters occasionally sampled the beverages is self-evident.

The Immigrants

America is almost unique among the nations. It is one of the few countries without a native population. All the people in America are of foreign parentage, save only the Indians. The only difference between the various people is the length of time they or their families have been here. Some trace their arrival to the first trip of the Mayflower and others to the last trip of the most modern passenger steamer.

The first vanguard of pioneers came to Texas without a particular destination in view. But in this little manual, we shall speak of those who settled at New Ulm, Industry, Frelsburg and Cat Spring, —which section in the early forties, comprised but one large settlement. On the arrival of new settlers, log houses grew up. As new comers chose to cast their lots with the new community, the pioneers turned out to help them erect their homes. The addition of a new home was marked by a house warming—that was the ceremony which welcomed the new comer into full community fellowship. A helping hand was extended to the new family until they could sow and reap a harvest. Fail crops never occurred. Cotton, corn, tobacco and other crops produced a heavy yield with very little cultivation. Often relatives, who had been here a couple of years, paid transportation charges for their kinsfolk from the fatherland to the "Home of the free and the brave". Seed was

loaned them when they arrived here. The older
residents showed their new friends where the best
fish could be caught, where the purest water
flowed, where the best and most luscious wild
fruit grew in abundance, and where the game was
most plentiful.

We must not forget that these men and women
who walked across the narrow ship's plank to the
mainland at Galveston or some other seaport,
landed hopeful but confused with bundles of misconceptions as heavy as their luggage upon their
backs and that these simple, rough handed people
are the ancestors of our descendants, the fathers
and mothers of our children, the ones who now
occupy the center of the governmental stage; and
that we owe these hardy pioneers, who sanctified
Texas soil with their sweat and blood, a debt of
gratitude which we can not pay at their graves—we
can only pass on to the future some service in acknowledgment of that which the past has rendered us.

A great deal has been written about the lawlessness of the pioneer days but we have no reason to
believe that it was worse then than now. It is true
that there was no restriction on a man's right to
carry all arsenal that he saw fit. There were occasional shooting scrapes but otherwise acts of violence were much rarer in proportion to
population than they are today; and with respect
to obedience to laws in general, the record of
those days would put the present day to shame.
There was also a great deal more respect for the
rights of others then than there is today and this

was naturally the case as each man was prepared to enforce his rights, if called upon, and the result was that it was very rarely called for.

Let us glory in the title of American citizen! It matters not whether this is the land of our birth or the land of our adoption. It is the land of our destiny! Here we intend to live and here we hope to die.

Victor Niemeyer Knippa, Texas.

New Ulm Had an Interesting Beginning

By A. Haubold, Waco, Texas.

The eldest settler of the old town of New Ulm that I learned to know was Julius Holmig. My father, Fritz Haubold, acquired Mr. Holmig's residence by purchase, after which the Holmig family moved to the Bernard Prairie, occupying the farm that later became the property of Robert Weber. Still later, Holmig moved to Fredericksburg. Adolf Richter conducted the first tin shop in the building later occupied by Robert Wagner. Well do I remember the nick-name given to Mr. Wagner because of his over-zealousness in extending courtesy to his customers. He was known among his friends as Mr. Schoen-Diener.

Charles Kessler was my first teacher at New Ulm, He was succeeded by Otto Daub. Robert Boerner also taught school in New Ulm for a short while on the second floor of his building. For a certain length of time, we had to do without a teacher in town during which time, we went to Mr. Prause's school which was in the timberland near the Carl Krause or Kroll farm. After this, Judge Teichmueller taught at New Ulm for a period of four or five years. Prior to becoming a teacher, Judge Teichmueller resided at Post Oak Point on the Farenholdt farm. I saw him many a time drive a yoke of oxen into town hitched to a slide, his wife riding in the slide, while he walked alongside of his ox-team. After resigning his tutorship of the New Ulm school, Mr. Teichmueller devoted his time to the study of law in the building that had been vacated by Mr. Dohmann who had manufactured cigars therein. Mr. Charles Ernst, Sr., succeeded Mr. Teichmueller as teacher. The school house was located about a mile from the old town on the Kotzebue farm, later known as the Merten place. After Mr. Kessler withdrew from the profession of teaching, he opened a store in the building which later was used for a kitchen by the New Ulm Turn-Verein.

Many of the early pioneers of New Ulm removed to High Hill. Among those I knew were Charles Kessler, Robert Wolters, Sr., Ebeling, Flato, Adolf Richter, Chas. Korth, Ernst Korth, Yeager and several more whose names I do not recall. Luescher operated a small brewery near the D. Schweke gin in the timber near a never-failing spring. Thir brewery was in operation long before Wm. Hagemann and Haemmerlein brewed beer in the old town.

The old town boasted of a so-called Schuetzen-Verein (military organization). I remember the members wore uniforms of a light green color. August Klump was Justice of the Peace for several years. Old man Poth, Ludwig Wink and Robert Weber were blacksmiths. Weber sold out to Ludwig Kuehn and opened another shop adjacent to Wangemann & Becker's store. Loevenstein Bros, also conducted a mercantile business adjacent to

Weber's blacksmith shop. Nicolaus Kieselbach was a very successful pioneer carpenter and has the building of many substantial residences and others buildings as well as the erection of gin buildings to his credit. All the lumber used in the construction of a house, including sills, scantlings, plaids, rafters, girders and cross beams were split from post oak trees and hewn out with a broad ax. Shingles were also split into round post oak logs. Franz Pille, another pioneer who was a miller in the old country, took up carpentry here in the land of his adoption. Mr. Daughtry offered him a half league of land as compensation for building him a double log house. Mr. Pille, however, refused to accept the offer but expressed a willingness to erect the double log house on condition that Mr. Daughtry pay him $150.00 for his services. Mr. Daughtry agreed to the proposition, whereupon work on the building was commenced. Mr. Pille hewed all the logs and fitted them with a broadax.

Alter all the logs had been given their proper shape and hauled to the building site, house raising was in order in which all settlers residing within a radius of ten or more miles participated. It was a housewarming festival and greatly enjoyed by the settlers. Later when Mr. Pille built his own house, he followed the same procedure and had his house raised with the help of his next neighbors. It was a big feast for all the participants. At night a bunch of mischievously inclined settlers tore the logs apart and scattered them to winds much to the chagrin of the owner. Perhaps this prank was committed as a joke and for the purpose of having an excuse for returning the next day to help in reraising the frame work. Anyway the grooves and edges had to be recut to insure a snug fit at the corners.

Ferdinand Wolters, saddle and harness maker, was succeeded by Charles Ernst. When Fritz Haubould opened his wheelwright shop in the old town of New Ulm, there were no saw mills in existence. All the material needed for the making of plows, wagons, ox-yokes and so forth had to be split from logs and then hewn and shaped with a broadax to a certain size and then sawed out by means of a hand saw. Later Sternenberg erected a saw mill near our timberland at Star Hill. Right here, permit me to interpolate that although I have seen lots and lots of work oxen on duty and have occasionally driven an ox team myself, I have never before or since seen an ox team to equal the one owned by Max Sternenberg. The team was composed of six or eight yoke of oxen hitched to a two-wheeled cart, a special make of cart suited to the dragging of logs to the saw mill. Mr. Sternenberg never left the seat of his two-wheeled monster cart except when he was about to fasten the hooks to the log. He could drive his long string of oxen around trees and wind and circle about in the timber like a snake with nothing to guide the team except a long whip and his voice by which he commandeered the oxen from his seat. The leaders were of a raven black color and a dead match and were endowed with almost human intelligence. At the driver's command the off ox would step or jump over the log so that the team would straddle it to enable Mr. Sternenberg to sink the huge iron hooks into the log and drag it to the saw mill. Although a yoke of oxen was comparatively cheap in those days, Mr, Sternenberg refused to accept an offer of $500.00 for the black leaders.

A. Haubold Waco, Texas.

My father, Fritz Haubold, whom I assisted in the wheel-wright business, received the order for a pair of new wheels to fit the monster two-wheeled cart. The wheels were fourteen feet in diameter and when finished were too large to be taken out of the shop without enlarging the door. Realizing that it was cheaper to take them apart and complete the job on the outside of the shop, we chose the latter. All the iron parts of the plows were made by blacksmiths, not only by those of New Ulm but also by A. Braesaecke of Cat Spring, Zimmerscheidt and Gottlob Moeckel and also by Moeckel at Frelsburg and others in the neighboring towns and settlements. We stocked about 250 plows in a year and many of them had wooden mouldboards. Then, too, we had to repair and build ox-wagons, ox-yokes and at a later date, we built light wagons for horses and mules; also hacks, carriages and buggies. The old shop was also used for a dance hall as there was no other dance hall in town. Later my father built a new shop and had it arranged so that it could easily be converted into a dance hall or opera house The building was equipped with a stage or rostrum supplied with screens and so forth. The home talent, dramatic club or local theater troupe, or by whatever name people chose to call it, was composed of the following members: Professor Tielau, director; Miss Selma Witte, Miss Bertha Witte, Miss Lina Haubold, Miss Natalia Haubold, F. Haubold, Chas. May, Theodore Wolters and A. Haubold. Generally they staged but one play a month but would assist other dramatic clubs staging plays at Cat Spring, Industry, Shelby, Millheim, Bluff and Brenham.

The New Ulm Turn Verein was famous far and wide for its hospitality and for its liberality in providing amusements for children. The first children's feast given under the auspices of the Turn Verein at New Ulm was arranged by my father and others in the year 1859, which is as far back as I can remember. There were also Schuetzen feasts (target practice) and fourth of July celebrations, of which I still have faint recollections.

Pfeifen Lehmann, an old settler of new New Ulm, was a very interesting individual. He served in the civil war as a substitute for Ernst Wangemann. His two sons, Bruno and Emil, constituted the town band. One played the violin and the other the accordion. Another old time musician of considerable reputation was a Mr. Motel, who furnished the music for many dances and parties. He was a clarinet virtuoso and would play from eight p.m. until sun rise next morning all by himself.

Adolph Peschel built the first hotel and dance hall at New Ulm. He sold out to Mr, Kiesel who in turn transferred his interest to Wm. Hagemann, who remodeled the building and converted same into a tomato cider and grape wine distillery and brewery.

The old ox-teamsters in the days of long ago, I used to know were: Wm. Voelkel, Sr., John Meyer, Otto Henkhaus, Diedrich Stein, John Brod and others, all of whom have long since folded their tents and departed to that haven of rest from whence no traveler ever returneth.

The old town also boasted of a splendid singing club under the able leadership of Mr. Dittmar; who also held the position of county surveyor.

George Brune operated a tread-mill on the farm now occupied by the Scherpig's, and also ginned cotton—not by horsepower, nay—ox-power being used. Regardless of ownership the wild steers roaming at large in the timberland, were rounded up and driven onto the crane-wheel and encouraged to jump, kick and balk as much as they liked. Of course their efforts to break loose put the machinery in motion and enabled the gin owner to utilize their power. After using the steers for a week they were released and a fresh supply driven in to take their place.

Lindemann owned and operated an outfit of like character in the timberland on the farm now occupied by Adolf Bastían. The gin building was later bought by F Haubold, torn down by N. Kieselbach and re-erected and annexed to Haubold's shop to provide more room for tools etc.

Mr. Sturm operated a wheelwright on the farm now owned by Gerhard Muench. A Mr. Herbrig was his assistant.

Mr. Bittner's residence was located opposite the old town's schoolhouse but I do not recall his profession, if any he followed.

The old, genial Thomas Wangler, a native of Tyrol, Switzerland, occupied a log cabin residence in the central part of town. Although an old man in years, he was young in mind and body and preferred to keep company with the youngsters of the neighborhood. Never did the youngsters do a mischievous prank without first consulting and obtaining advice and assistance from their spry old leader.

After the cessation of hostilities between the states, and upon the return of the veteran soldiers to their families, the inhabitants agreed to stage a 4th of July celebration in the settlement which furnished so many able bodied soldiers. F. Haubold's wheelwright shop was quickly transformed into a festival hall which practically was all the preparation necessary. The day dawned bright and warm with a mild breeze blowing from the coast which made it an ideal day for outdoor rest and recreation. Several hundred guests had arrived early in the morning and kept milling around the grandstand where the war veterans had assembled to tell of their hardships and privations during their service in the confederate army. However, the festive spirit, the friendly cooperation and the feeling of brotherly love was still lacking until noon, at which time the ox-team caravan bringing refreshments from the cellars of Mr, Schulte's brewery of Houston, arrived. The teamsters, fully aware of their belated arrival, parked their canvas covered wagons in a circle in the center of the business section, unyoked their steers and allowed them to roam about at will. The celebration lasted several days after which the teamsters collected their teams, yoked them up and proceeded on to their final destination at Bastrop. Perhaps it is not amiss to state that the guests were plainly dressed in homespun and wore, if any at all, bachelor shoes laced up with rawhide strings.

F. Haubold Pioneer Of New Ulm, Texas.

Pioneer Physicians of New Ulm

Along with the early pioneers came two physicians. One of whom, Dr. Thomson, a one-armed man, committed self-destruction near Kessler's lake soon after the cessation of the war between the States because, it is said, of the worry over his financial losses and separation from his family.

Dr. A. Hanke, another prominent and successful physician of the early pioneer days, who could well afford to boast of an eventful and adventurous life, accompanied by his young wife, came to New Ulm with the first influx of German immigrants. Born in Austria of German parentage, he studied medicine in Prague and later took a post graduate course in Vienna. He was a member of a monastic order, however, the monastic life, ways and belief were not to his liking and try as hard as he might, he could not conceal his love and admiration that he had for a young woman, also an inmate of the convent in which he practiced medicine and surgery. The doctrine of the Roman Catholic Church forbade their marrying each other. The young physician fell desperately in love with the young lady, who trying as hard as she might could not resist smiling at her lover whenever their eyes met. Taking advantage of a propitious moment, the pair decided to disrobe, elope and sail for America where they could forever live happily together as man and wife. The young couple directed their footsteps to Texas, settling at New Ulm at an early day—the exact date is not available; and here they prospered. Their matrimonial union was without issue, however, they adopted two orphan children and reared them to splendid citizens.

In his declining days, Dr. Hanke moved to Nelsonville, where he purchased a modest little home and lived the life of a recluse until about five years prior to his death when he provided passage for his grand-nephew, Charles Ebert, now a prosperous farmer of Kenney. Dr. Neal, an Englishman, and Dr. E. Becker, a native of Germany, came a couple of years later to this section. Dr. Neal settled a mile south of the present town of Frelsburg, while Dr. E. Becker erected the first brick residence a mile east of Frelsburg in the timberland. Dr. Becker sold his home to F. A. Laake and it is now the property of Hugo Schuette. Ben H. Neal, son of Dr. Neal, came into possession of the Dr. Neal homestead.

Pioneers Had Few Comforts of Life

The interior as well as the exterior of a log cabin, such as were in vogue three-quarters of a century ago, can not be accurately described to convey a lasting impression on the minds of those who must of necessity get the thought from the printed page. Think of a family occupying a room sixteen feet square, in which space had to be provided for the stove or fireplace, dining table, cupboard, bedstead, trundle bed and benches. The old-fashioned handmade bedsteads were built to correspond in height with the dining table in order to furnish sufficient space underneath for the trundle bed, small trunks, boxes and so forth. Mattresses were stuffed with shredded corn shucks, hay or moss and placed on the bare slats of the bedstead. In course of time, the bed would become as hard as the floor, if not properly made up every morning. Windows were set into the walls four feet above the floor while doors were made so low that on entering the room, people had to stoop to avoid bumping their heads. A sorrowful candle or grease lamp, which, when burning would soon fill the room with smoke of an unpleasant oder, furnished the dim light. On the wall next to the door were racks fastened to the logs for the settler's guns, hung so as to admit their easy removal in case of emergencies. When someone hallooed at the front gate and failed to give an account of himself, the light would be extinguished. One of the men of the house would slip out of the rear door, gun in hand, while the others would guard the front entrance. The party who had made his exit out of the rear door generally did the shooting if there was an occasion for it but that was rarely, if ever, the case.

In the summer time, the settlers usually ate their dinner and supper under the giant shade trees that encircled the dwelling. And as each settler had a pack of hounds or cur dogs, it was not uncommon for them to settle their disputes beneath the table and thus unconsciously provoke a breach of peace among the diners.

As water wells were practically unknown prior to 1870, water had to be hauled from the creeks in barrels, fastened on the top of a slide drawn by oxen. On the top side of the barrel, two staves were cut out in the middle to admit the passage of a small bucket or a long handled gourd to dip the water.

Ready-to-wear garments, including socks and underwear, were not carried in stock by the merchants. The calico string, tied about the leg over the hose below the knee to hold the hose up, gave way to elastic and later to the modern garter and hose supporter.

On Sunday mornings, men would be out bright and early in their shirt sleeves that were held up by bright sleeve garters, grandmother knitted. Men were not particularly about their wearing apparel and treasured their handmade suits made of

Pioneers Had Few Comforts of Life

homespun material all the more because of the durability of the fabric of which it was made. They cared little for color or style and had no special liking for cologna or face cream. They valued the assoefidita[2] bag and believed in larding their hair on Sundays.

The young men would go out to see their best girl Sunday morning and remain until supper. They would help their fiancees clean the yard of leaves and trash, help her catch a rooster for the noon meal, peal potatoes and lend her a helping hand when and wherever possible. Late in the evening, he would assist her in milking the cows, rope the calves off and carry milk pails into the house. Off and on, he would present her with a nice apple or some other token of affection. After their matrimonial union, separation or divorces were seldom.

Texas Longhorn Steer

---

2 Small bags stuffed with pungent herbs and other ingredients to ward off disease and evil spirits, and to treat asthma, colds, or other respiratory ailments.

Learned physicians were few and far between until about the year 1880, when more doctors began locating in the small interior towns, where they could visit their patients daily and prescribe for them in a scientific way.

Mrs. August Klump,

Oldest Living Pioneer of Austin County

Mrs. August Klump, nee Fehrenkamp, is probably the oldest living pioneer in Austin County. Mr. and Mrs. August Klump settled in the timberland near New Ulm in the year 1854. Mrs. Klump was ninety-seven years old in March, 1930. Unfortunately she lost her eye-sight a score of years ago which shut off the beauties of nature to her vision and made her feel very lonesome at times. She lives with her daughter, Mrs. Emilie Blaschke at Cat Spring, and is the mother of the following named living children: William and Otto of Stonewall County; Louis of Bellville; Ignatz of Goliad County; Ernest of Rockhouse; Mrs. Emilie Blaschke of Cat Spring; Mrs. Henrietta Hines of Greenvine; and Albert Klump of Rosebud.

Mrs. Elizabeth Peebles
Close Rival To Mrs. August Klump

Mrs. Elizabeth Peebles, nee Spies, is still active at the advanced age of ninety-six years. Mrs. Peebles is a native of Switzerland but came to Texas long before Texas ceased to be a republic. She loves to reminiscence of the pioneer days and of events that occurred prior to the civil War. She lives with her daughter, Mrs. M. N. Wood at Welcome.

The Dentler Family

John George Dentler in company with Lorenz Mueller, Lorenz Sailer and other Swabians came to Duff's settlement in 1849. Later Dentlar built a log cabin near the home of Jack Rinn near a Creek which still bears his name but more recently known as Post Oak Point Creek. The Creek was much larger and swifter three-quarters of a century ago than now. It is the same creek in which Arthur W. Kuehn unearthed a fossil of the prehistoric ages about three years ago.

Dentler mowed grass on the prairies between Industry and New Ulm with a hand scythe for the wage of one dollar per acre. The hay was hauled away on a hand made wagon and when loaded to capacity, nothing but the tongue, made from a post oak sappling, to which the oxen were hitched, could be seen. Visitors from Duff's settlement and Austin's colony would occasionally inspect the hay-loads, ride around the wagon, exclaiming: "I be darned if it doesn't look like a monster sea turtle."

Surviving John George Dentler are two sons: L. Dentler of Wallis, who is eighty-two years of age, and M. Dentler of Taylor, who is eighty-four years of age.

Reminiscences of a Native Austin Countian

E. M. Knolle, son of Mr. and Mrs. Ernst Knolle, early pioneers of Industry, was born September 23, 1847, in an old primitive log cabin near the present site of Industry. When the Knolle family came to Texas, and subsequently to Industry, there were but three houses in the wide open prairie. The houses were built of logs with openings between them which had to be filled in with moss, sticks and mud to reduce the ventilation to a minimum. The work of closing the cracks provided much sport for the barefoot boy, who, by nature, is endowed with the art of making mud pies.

Mr. Knolle, although now in his eighty-third year, has a vivid recollection of what transpired in his boyhood days. The first school teacher he ever learned to know was named Obrien or Obryant. Despite the numerous draw backs the pioneers had to contend with, Mr. Knolle acquired the best education possible in a country that was just being settled by a motley, but highly intelligent and thrifty class of people which accounts for his social and financial success in life.

Prior to his reaching majority, he joined the ox-wagon caravan, plying between Industry, Brenham and Hempstead, the latter being a railroad station, where Gustav Maetze[3] was holding the position of railroad agent. The teamsters received Five Dollars for transporting a bale of cotton from Industry to Hempstead. On their return they loaded freight for merchants at Brenham and Industry at the rate of one dollar per hundred pounds. Among those who served in the same capacity and who participated in the ox-wagon brigade were: August Roesler, who is still living at the age of ninety-two, C. A. Weige and James Shelburne, deceased.

In the late sixties, he joined his father, Ernst Knolle, in the mercantile business at Industry and two years later traded his interest in the business for his father's farm, and although, harvesting a bountiful crop, he decided to re-enter the mercantile business and opened a store on a lot he had previously purchased from Mrs. Wangemann, where for several decades, he conducted one of the most flourishing mercantile establishments of all inland towns of Texas. In 1913, he sold out, lock, stock and barrel. After a short rest and business recess he and Mrs., Knolle located at New Ulm, where in addition to serving as a

3 Gustav Maetze had been a teacher in Germany and because of his political views left and went to Texas. One day he was found wandering the prairie on Horseback by Ferdinand Engelking of Millheim and became the teacher in the first high school in Texas established there. cf. "The Engelking Letters" by Flora von Roeder ISBN: 978-3949197086 and "The Millheim and Cat Spring Pioneers" by James V. Woodrick and Stephen A. Engelking ISBN: 9781999869120

telephone operator, he conducted a small grocery and confectionery until the infirmities of old age crept upon him..

Mr. Knolle is still very much interested in all kinds of business affairs and gets much pleasure and satisfaction leafing through Bradstreet or Dunn, informing himself of the financial standing of the present day business men and of his own commercial rating.

Mr, Knolle's father owned and operated the first steam tannery on the banks of Pastoren Creek under the management of Carl Bastian. He also erected the first steam cotton gin, grist, saw and flour mill in Austin County, if not in Texas. The settlers were induced and persuaded to plant a certain acreage to wheat, which they did.

The first year the wheat crop yielded abundantly to the joy and satisfaction of the settlers; but the second year, however, was an utter fail crop because of the wheat being susceptible to rust and not adapted to the climatic conditions here.

Spurned by the fact that immediately upon his landing here many of the settlers busied themselves mowing grass with a hand scythe at the ridiculous wage of one dollar per acre, the senior Knolle purchased and operated the first mowing machine on his farm ever brought to Austin County, if not to Texas. The mower was a new invention and drawn by an ox-team; and, although, three men. testified to having seen the mower in operation on the Ernst Knolle farm, none remembered accurately the size or shape of the knife or blade which was entirely different from those now in vogue.

The Messrs Franz Schramm and Jacob Wuertz owned in partnership the first sausage grinder and meat stuffer ever brought to Austin County. Prior to the invention of the meat chopper and sausage stuffer much oi the meat was salted down or cut up in shreds and smoked-dry.

Glimpses of Pioneer Life

Born in Pritzwalk, Germany, the son of a forester, my father was seized with the wanderlust in 1848, landing in New York the same year. Instead of proceeding on to Texas, as he had intended, he acceded to the wishes of an Irishman, who befriended him, and accompanied him to Quebec, where he for two years worked at the shoemaker's trade. After accumulating fifty dollars in cash, he started out in search of an uncle whose former place of abode was in New Burg, Pennsylvania. Not being familiar with the pronunciation of English names, he requested that he be directed to Nave Burg, but in vain. The settlers along his route of travel shook their heads, assuring him that they were not acquainted with a locality or postoffice town of that name and suggested that he proceed farther down into the interior of the country. At Philadelphia, he had his belongings re-checked to Galveston, where he joined other immigrants on their way to Cat Spring. After taking temporary employment with Dr. Bergmann, he worked at the shoemaker's trade off and on until his marriage to Dr. Bergmann's niece, in 1852, after which they purchased fifty acres of land near the present village of Mentz, Colorado County. There they built an unpretentious log cabin and engaged in farming. The first five years of their married life was of an adventurous nature and bare of luxuries and all comforts of life. In 1860, the Southern Pacific built its terminal at Alleyton, which provided a little more convenience and comfort to the isolated farmers since it brought their shipping point so much nearer to their homes. In 1861, the threatened eruption between the North and the South became a reality. The whole country was in a tumult and starvation seemed inevitable to the settlers and their scantily clad and poorly fed families. Some of the settlers shouldered their guns and marched off in defense of their beloved South, while others were employed by the government at Houston, and still others went out hiding to escape the conscript chasers and then returning to their families after nightfall and helping them till the soil by the light of the moon in hopes of making a crop to sustain them. Let us for a moment imagine how the pioneers suffered plowing in stumpy land by the light of the moon with, only a partially trained yoke of oxen hitched to a hand made plow which would break the long whip-shaped roots of live oak saplings and cause the roots to rebound with tremendous force, striking the plowman across his legs and not infrequently cutting the skin and drawing blood.

Conscript chasers were the most despised individuals in the state. These scouts, as we shall refer to them here, spent much of their time hunting for those out hiding to escape service in the army. They would sometimes visit the farmhouses and turn everything topsyturvy. On one occasion, the scouts accosted mother and her little brood in an effort to obtaining information as to the whereabouts of her husband and neighbors. Mother calmly answered, speaking in German: "In den Krieg", meaning in the war, whereupon the scouts requested that she repeat the words which she had said, and she did putting stress and emphasis upon the word "Krieg." "Do you mean to say they are hiding in the creek?", asked the one nearest her. She nodded in the affirmative. "Thank you." shouted the scouts, galloping away towards the creek in search of men they never found.

After four years of suffering and privations, the war ended. In the meantime, the children had grown older and stronger, making the selection of a larger acreage, affording more elbow room necessary. The fifty acre farm was sold at $150.00, after which my parents lived on the Leyedecker farm near Frelsburg as farm tenants until several years later when they acquired a homestead near Shaws Bend.

It was a bright moonlit night on August 24, 1869, when the stork delivered me to William and Mary Schmidt. There was a great and unusual commotion in the neighborhood as two brothers and six sisters had preceded me and when I let lose a yell announcing that I had arrived, all the mothers in the neighborhood called to give me the once over and such "to do" it was, with the comments of: "just like his father" and "do you think he will make good?" and there I lay winking and blinking. There were so many comments that I did not admire, that I broke out with another yell, which meant in baby language "rouse mit em" and wishing to exercise my lungs, I gave several more yells and then they splashed water over my face and chest and ordered a dose of camomile or fennel tea to quiet me down, but it only seemed to give an infantile jag and I raised more thunder. After that I was induced to partake of a good supper and I fell asleep; and on awakening the next morning, a nice warm bath finished off with starch or rice powder, so I decided to stay here and become a useful citizen. Although somewhat gifted in the musical line, I never learned to play on the linoleum. I took all of my lessons on the dirt floor and since we lived near a fresh water stream, I submitted to an emersion quite often in order to look my best.

About the year, 1873, my father and other new comers started hauling lumber from Spring Creek. Often as many as ten ox-teams went after lumber together, driving caravan fashion and signaling each other by popping the ox whip. On their return trip, they would put up camp on the wide expanse near the Crump ferry on the Brazos River. Not infrequently, other teamsters joined them at the camp and befriended them as the sequel shows.

After supper, the oxen were hobbled, belled and turned loose to take care of themselves. The teamsters engaged in all kinds of amusements including pranks of various kinds. On one occasion, the teamsters chose to play hide and seek in the bright moon light, and started counting out the seeker by repeating the rhyme: "Eeney, meeny weeney, moo" and so forth, and the last one not counted out was the seeker, who, like an ostrich, would hide his head—not in the sand—but in the canvas covered wagon until all had found a snug hiding place. Then he started out finding them. On this particular occasion, the seekership fell on a Mr. Burger, a jolly good fellow. He started out looking behind the wagons, behind the big trees, bushes and so forth, and finally he marched along the edge of the prairie when all of a sudden, he spied a black object moving rapidly in the opposite direction. Burger followed in all possible speed but the object outdistanced him and was lost to view. Feeling discouraged, he was on the verge of returning to camp when a piece of a rotten limb fell on his head, attracting his attention and on looking up the tree against which he was leaning, he spied a large black lump about fifteen feet above the ground. Elated over his discovery, he shouted: "I spy you, John, I spy you, Jim!" and kept calling the names of all of his companions but there was no response. "I betcher, I'll make you come down from your hiding place," he shouted as he removed his shoes, preparatory to climbing the tree. On reaching his objective, he reached out his hand to grasp the foot of his alleged playmate. He released his hold quicker than it takes to write it for it wasn't a man's foot—it was a bear. More than an hour elapsed before all participants in the nocturnal frolic had assembled to assist Burger in killing the beast that had been a menace to the Crump Ferry campers for many months.

How Industry Got Its Name.

The founding of Industry on the banks of West Mill Creek, Austin County, Texas, by F. Ernst and family and Chas. Fordtran, the first vanguard of German immigrants that settled there in 1831, the hardships and privations they endured and the history they made for the State and Nation, has been given a prominent place in the State adopted School text books; and it has been told and retold so often until it has become a vital part of the historic old town itself.

F. Ernst and family accompanied by Chas. Fordtran landed at Harrisburg on April 1st, 1831, at which place they took passage on a private schooner that carried them many miles inland on the road leading to San Antonio via Bastrop. On the Banks of Mill Creek, among beautiful hills and fascinating valleys, they found a few white sellers with whom they cast their lot for better or worse. There, after ordering their baggage unloaded, they started building their rude log house, hexagon shaped, windowless and covered with a thatched roof.

The Ernst Home was erected, within a stone's throw off the Houston-San Antonio-Bastrop road, traces of which still exist. The Indians would frequently travel this road on their expedition tours to their trading posts where they would barter skins of animals for trinkets, guns and ammunition. On passing the residence, they would go inside, inspect the cooking vessels, eat everything that was good for the stomach, take the guns off their racks, examine them very closely, replace them, and then continue their way without molesting the inmates.

B. E. Knolle, Industry, oldest practicing physician in Austin County,

Frequently the settlers subsisted for weeks on smoked beef, roasted game and herbs. Corn was very scant and sold, if there was any at all, at $3.00 per bushel. Crushing corn and grinding it into meal required considerable skill, perseverance and patience, since the work of pounding it was a very tedious task, and was usually accomplished

How Industry Got Its Name.

by crushing the same between two large rocks. On one occasion, Mr. Ernst gave a thick woolen mantel in exchange for twenty bushels of corn and felt happy about it. The fact that Mr. Ernst's home was near a much traveled road of the State, made it a kind of rendezvous and favorite inn for explorers as well as for new settlers.

Often it happened that travelers arrived at the Ernst Hotel with insufficient funds to pay for their board and lodging. Some of those early explorers were noblemen, high social rank in the country of their birth. None, however, were turned away because of lack of funds or simplicity of, dress. Some of these explorers were anxious to reciprocate and remunerate the Ernst family for courtesies shown them. One of the travelers presented Mr. Ernst with a coffee mill, another left him a saddle horse, while still another remained long enough to teach him how to manufacture cigars since tobacco culture was very promising, the plants growing to an enormous height with leaves as large and wide as any produced in the East, Mr. Ernst soon mastered the art of manufacturing cigars and acquired a fair knowledge as to how to pack the finished product. As soon as the local demand was inadequate to the supply, Mr. Ernst would sew up his product in sacks of one thousand each and carry them on horseback to San Felipe where he sold them at twenty dollars per thousand. The inhabitants of San Felipe were so well pleased with their purchases that they called Mr. Ernst an industrious man. Later, when a statesman of prominence desired a good cigar,

He would call for an "Industry cigar" and that is why the town was given the name of "Industry".

When, in 1836, Mr. and Mrs Ernst Knolle arrived a t Industry, they found conditions more endurable. There were three houses one of which was occupied by three bachelor physicians, who conducted a small drugstore in addition to the practice of medicine. The building which they occupied also furnished hospital conveniences for the travelers. In the meantime, Mr. Ernst remodeled his hexagon shaped residence and converted same into a larger structure, providing private quarters for the family in addition, to the dance hall and hotel reservations. In 1837, more settlers arrived in Austin County, settling within a radius

First Postoffice Building of Industry, Texas, 1838.

of ten miles of Industry, all of whom received their mail at Industry, which became a post office town in the year 1838, with Mr Sieper as first

How Industry Got Its Name.

postmaster. A portion of the old stone building is still in a fair state of preservation and is now being used by Otto Schroeder for a smokehouse.

This old building, Industry's first postoffice, is the only landmark left of the. original pioneer buildings viewed and admired by the Indians while on their retreat from their hunting-grounds; and the narrow private road that leads up the Ernst original farmstead reflects the only trace of the Houston-Bastrop-San Antonio state road which in the days of long, long ago was the only thoroughfare of prominence in this section of the state.

G F, Knolle. Uncle Sam's, Faithful Servitor as Postmaster of Industry for the past 38 consecutive years.

After the termination of the civil war, more people, more capital and more and better conveniences found their way into Austin County, and prospects, although by no means bright or brilliant, changed for the better. Starvation no longer stared the settlers in the face. New buildings sprung up like mushrooms after a summer rain. There was no longer need for the dance hall and hotel in the valley, consequently it was torn down and replaced with a modest farm building where hopes were born; where death took its toll and which is still occupied by four grandsons who marvel at the undaunted courage of their forbears who carved a beautiful settlement out of an untamed wilderness; and as a matter of pride, patriotism and filial love, they forever cherish the exact spot where a century ago, their grandparents laid the foundation of the First German settlement of Texas.

Ere the elapse of another century, Father Time will have finished writing the last chapter "Finis" across the doors of the old Ernst homestead, the builder of which led the way, while others followed his footsteps.

J. H. Petter. Superintendent of Public Instruction, Austin County

The School House

Most of the settlers were latinists and highly educated people who had left the land of their birth in order to escape the yoke of tyranny that deprived them of their freedom of life and encroached upon their personal liberties; and, rather than submit to and endure the poverty that they and their children would irrevocably fall heir to and lest fresh hostilities between the nations of Europe might automatically get them mixed up in things they did not like, they directed their journey to America, the land that promised them unlimited opportunities and personal freedom. Upon their arrival here, their first thoughts were given to the education of their children as most of the settlers had a great many. When more settlers arrived, a Lite for a schoolhouse was selected as near the center of the population as possible. The close proximity to water, wood and an outlet were the only features taken into consideration. Upon the completion of the building, which in the present age would not pass the inspection for the requirements of a modern poultry house, the inhabitants assembled for the dedication ceremonies at which the employment of a teacher was discussed. An applicant or prospect for the tutorship was chosen on the strength of his skill in penmanship.

After the employment of a teacher, great excitement profiled in the community. The children were being supplied with books that the settlers brought with them from the land of their birth. Each child was given a slate and a stone pencil, often so short that it was, difficult for the beginner to hold it between its nimbly, wobbly fingers; and strange as it might seem, the teacher wasted more time teaching the pupils how to grasp the pencil or pen, than was necessary or advisable.

The pupils were required to write on both sides of their slate. When erasures became necessary, they would moisten their slates with saliva and wipe it clean with their sleeves. Beginners were permitted to enlist the help of older pupils in furnishing moisture for the slate cleaning process.

A day or so before the opening day of school, each family would hitch a pair of oxen to the end of a log and drag it to and from the school house to make a path. The trees bordering the path were blazed—that is, the bark was partially cut away so as to expose the white wood which would serve as a guide for the children and at the same time serving the purpose of a road sign or mile post.

At the intersection of two or more paths, the children waited for one another before proceeding to the next cross road and so on until the schoolhouse came in sight. If a neighbor's children were behind time, they would holler to announce their coming. In the event the first group of children were unwilling to wait, they would stick a four or five foot stick into the ground in the middle of the path and draw a line on the ground indicating to where the shade reached

The School House

when they left. By observing the distance the shade had receded since the mark was made, it was possible to estimate fairly accurately the distance the group was ahead and how much they had to accelerate their walk to overtake them. On cloudy days moist soil was dug up after which each child would implant the impression of his foot on it. By noting the freshness of the soil around the foot impression, the belated children would guess the distance the others were ahead. Scrutinizing the impressions of the footprints, most of the children could tell by whom it was made.

Nothing of grade teaching was known. The beginner was first taught addition, next subtraction, multiplication and division in regular order. A thorough knowledge of fractions and percentage entitled the pupil to graduation. During the war between the States, school teaching was temporarily suspended. It is indeed regretable that those of our men and women of school age in the two decades between 1855 and 1875 were denied the privilege of an education.

After the reconstruction days, the State government provided for public free schools and better qualified teachers were employed. About the year 1880, the State's apportionment per capita for the education of children of scholastic age amounted to $3.50 per scholastic, in comparison with $15.00 in 1930.

The thoroughness with which the subjects were taught in the pioneer days is partly responsible for the success of those who became their own tutor and built on the foundation received in the unpretentious cracker box schoolhouse, which will soon cease to be even a milestone or a landmark.

Teachers Who Taught Two Generations and Are Still Teaching

R. Regenbrecht   P.G. Saage   E.W. Kloss

A Prairie Fire

One of the most-exciting, appalling and dangerous calamities that constantly confronted the pioneers was the threatening and devastating prairie fire.

After the winter and spring rains, the water, if at all, drained down to the lowland or forest streams. The flow of water was very sluggish because of the thick coat of dry leaves and grass that held the water in check. The water that settled in the low places formed pools or sloughs that made the soil very boggy. By autumn, the moisture around the grass roots was all absorbed, leaving the grass a rustling mass. Then came the dangerous time on the prairie.

Late in the autumn, after the frost has seared everything, and the sweet potato crop has been harvested and stored in kilns about the premises, the tall dry grass and weeds were like tinder. Sometimes the fire was started accidentally but more frequently by careless persons who were bent on dislodging game. A spark from a camp fire or from a pipe often started a blaze that extended many miles, destroying much property before it was brought under control or checked.

A prairie fire at night is one of the most exciting, thrilling and sublimest sights any person may want to witness. Streams of light leap into the sky; tongues of flames dart hither and thither, hissing, roaring, singeing and crackling into broad sheets of splendid light that illuminates and flood the heavens until the sky itself seems on fire.

The settlers never felt sale in the autumn until there were furrows plowed around their farmsteads. The flames would seldom leap the plowed ground and if it did, it soon died for want of food. Sometimes the fire would divide and burn around the farm buildings, uniting again as it sped on.

The pioneers taught their children how to fight a prairie fire by means of wet gunny sacks; with the use ot shovels and by breaking up and tearing down fences and other fire traps. Some fire fighters in their endeavor to check and bring the fire under control, overtaxed their strength and collapsed from exhaustion. Some died as a direct result of their undue exertions while still others permanently injured and impaired their health for life.

In the daytime, the flames advanced much more slowly than, at night. Fires burn much faster at night than in the daytime, consequently a prairie fire at night can do more harm and destroy and cover a larger acreage in ten minutes than in half an hour of daylight. Probably for the same reason that sound travels farther and faster at night than in the day. It is an undeniable fact that conversation over the long distance telephone can be better carried on and understood at night than by day. Autoists also claim that their cars run smoother and swifter during the night time.

Of course learned men differ as to the cause of this phenomenon but they assure us that some difference in the atmosphere causes the differ-

A Prairie Fire

ence in the speed of a prairie fire at night[4]. The pioneers always burnt their brush after nightfall, a custom which is still adhered to by their scions. During the first years of their sojourn in Texas, the settlers built long stretches of brush fences around their premises to keep stock and wild animals out of their crops. These brush fences were excellent fire traps. After serving their purpose for a couple of years, they were frequently set on fire purposely to make room for a stake and rider zigzag rail fence. The old time rail fence in some localities in the timbered sections of this country still exists, more as a matter of curiosity or as a souvenir, than economy.

It was one of the chief sports of the children to walk along on the top rail of the fence long distances. Not infrequently, they would lose their balance, fall off and suffer serious bodily injury. When practicing this sport during cloudy weather or after a heavy dew or mist, they stood in danger of getting snake bit. The poisonous copperhead often took its nap on the top rail and when annoyed in its sleep would unfailingly insert its ven-

---

[4] "Higher ambient temperatures enable fuels to reach the heat of combustion more quickly. Temperature also contributes to fire intensity by reducing relative humidity. The higher the relative humidity, the slower a fuel will heat—moisture must be driven off before combustion temperature is reached. Generally, for every 20°F rise in temperature, relative humidity is decreased by half. As the relative humidity drops, fire intensity and rate of spread increase." (https://agrilifeextension.tamu.edu/library/disasters-safety/wildfire-behavior-and-emergency-response/)

omous fangs in the flesh of its alleged enemy. In many localities, at the present age, fences are being removed from around the growing crops.

In the cities, concrete highways and paved streets border magnificent residences and blooming flower yards, a sight that ought to remind the motorist of the debt of gratitude they owe the pioneer settlers, who enjoyed and obeyed the laws of nature instead of heeding the white-gloved hand of a policeman on one of our dangerous narrow crossings.

Breaking Oxen

Training oxen to draw the car, plow or wagon was one of the most cherished exercises of the young men during the pioneer days, because of the excitement and thrills it furnished.

Before the calves were old enough to be weaned, they were yoked together with light ox-bows. Their tails were firmly tied together so the innocent creatures could jump, lunge, kick, pitch and balk as much as they chose, but could not turn quickly and break their necks. Sometimes they were frightened out of their senses when they discovered that they were fastened together. Each calf learned that its tail was fastened to something but what it was that held it, it had no way of knowing for if it tried to turn its head either to the right or to the left, there was something that had never been there before and which, if the calves had had their way, would not have been there very long. The baby ox-team was exercised a little daily and it required months of training before they understood that which the strange and uncomfortable rigging meant, that locked them together. By the time, the baby ox-team was a year old, they could pull light carts, sleds and fence rails. At the age of three or four years, the ox-team was perfectly gentle and trained to obey the language of the driver. Often a single farmer had as many as four or five yokes in training—a regular cornfield college.

A rope tied to the yoke or to the horns of the ox, answered the purpose of a line by which the team was guided in case it ignored the command of the teamster. A skillful teamster could drive six yoke of trained oxen easily and turn sharp corners with astounding accuracy and rapidity. In justice to the uninitiated, we are compelled to interpolate here and now the fact that in cases of emergencies, three and four year-old steers and even old bulls and cows were pressed into service to complete the team. This practice, however, was never sanctioned by the old timers because of the torture and cruel treatment to such animals.

The "nigh" ox pulled on the left and the "off" ox on the right side of the chain between them which hooked into the yoke. In the early days, the prairie grass grew several feet high and its long fibrous roots were as tough as those of Bermuda grass. A good prairie breaking team consisted of five or six yoke of oxen. The oxen are now being shipped to towns and cities to be slaughtered and manufactured into bologna sausage and sold at the corner grocery as one of the main delicatessen. Tractors take the place of the oxen on the farm to do the pulling.

Entertainment

A diversion which followed the breaking of the prairie in a new country as inevitably and surely as the building of the little cracker-box schoolhouse and stake and rider zigzag rail fence was the annual "Volksfest" as it was colloquially called. They were easy to get up in pioneer days when respite from the hard job of making an independent and carefree living was infrequent. The settlers would come early and stay late. None were ever questioned whether they came a foot, on horseback or riding in a slide or sitting on a rawhide drawn by a yoke of oxen. Their presence was sufficient evidence that they had come.

Each settler made it a point to entertain once a year or oftener if social conditions warranted it Often the womenfolk would be cleaning the house when the sight of bare floors would suggest an opportune time for a frolic and a member of the family would then mount a horse and set out to give the bids.

The guests did not mind if they did not receive their invitations from the host and hostess and would help pass around by word of mouth that a dance and social was to take place at Henry Burger's place on Saturday night. The hostess did not even have to make a trip to town for refreshments. With plenty cornmeal in the pantry and a good supply of smoked meat in the smokehouse, a keg of wine in the cellar and a two-gallon jug of snake medicine on the mantel shelf, she was well fortified. Nor did she have to rent chairs for the occasion as long boards were brought in from the barn lot, spliced at intervals on a chair and covered with folded quilts to serve as seat cushions.

When the guests arrived, somehow the girls always became segregated in the front room while the boys stood awkwardly and uncomfortably on the front porch. It took a courageous chap to make the initial move in the selection of a partner. Sometimes he merely beckoned with a stubby forefinger from the doorway to the lady of his choice, but she accepted as gracefully as if he had bowed gallantly before her.

Hunting Game

It was, perhaps, fortunate that the pioneer's muzzle loader shotgun did not bear its load farther than thirty yards with any degree of certainty, otherwise the game might have been extinct ere this. Rifles bore their bullets farther but their skillful operation required considerable practice and marksmanship upon the part of the hunter. Then, too, the reloading process required time, patience and a steady nerve, especially when the object was a big buck that would raise his hind leg and kick on hearing the report of the hunter's gun. Ordinarily ammunition was not wasted on game beyond the lurc of the hunter. Deer and turkeys were plentiful practically all the year around, while geese and ducks spent only the cooler seasons here and were more highly treasured because of their heavy coat of soft downy feathers than for the meat they furnished. The settlers would go out on a still hunt, that is without dogs, preferably in the morning when the dew was on the grass or after a light shower. In the autumn and winter seasons, the ground was covered with leaves to a depth of several inches which made it impossible for hunters to walk as stealthily as a cat in an effort to avoid detection by the game because of the crackling noise of the leaves when trod upon. Deer and turkey would roam about in flocks and there would often be as many as thirty or more in a single herd. Turkey gobblers were shot off their roosts in early spring. The hunter would rise before daylight, walk into the forest, sit down and wait until his attention was attracted by the gobbling. Frequently as many as a dozen turkey gobblers started their gobbling contemporaneously. The hunter would slip up to the roost nearest him, bag the game and reach home in time for breakfast.

About the year 1880, headlights first came into use which enabled the hunter to locate game through the reflection of the animal's eyes. This mode of hunting was soon restricted and confined to ones own premises because of the numerous calves, colts, sheep and other domestic animals that were mistaken for deer and killed.

About the same time, the first breech loader shot gun was introduced and with it the Winchester repeating rifle while the pump gun made its appearance here about the year 1890.

Locating Bee Trees

To enable the readers to better understand and appreciate the subject matter of this article, it is necessary that we preface same with an explanation. The sons of the early settlers would, in their unoccupied moments, assemble in groups for the purpose of exploring the country adjacent to their homes, going a little farther each time they went out; and, after a time, each ventured to penetrate the dense forest unaccompanied. After familiarizing themselves with the direction the streams flowed, their sources and outlets, and fastening the locations of hills, valleys, thickets, large trees, monster grapevines, and other symbols, not made by man or his money, they would venture going out hunting alone. The guns they owned were of the muzzle loading type and often undependable because of the exposure of the percussion caps to moisture. Sometimes when they crippled a wild animal, the excitement ran high and in their endeavor to reload their guns, with all possible haste, the wooden ramrod broke to pieces. When in this unexpected predicament, they frequently preferred a good run to a bad stand.

In early summer, when the crops were laid by, the boys would hunt for bee trees. Nature provided dwelling places for the insects as well as for rodents and so forth. Squirrels would build their nests to rear their young of moss in the tree tops, but would spend the winters in hollow trees in which they had previously stored an abundant supply of acorns, hickories and pecans. Ten per cent of the trees in the unoccupied forests, never before traversed by civilized people, were hollow either at the stem, middle or top ends; and supplied with knot holes, oblong or circular shaped. The hollow at the base was usually occupied by rabbits, o'possums, snakes and skunks; the hollow in the middle part of the tree was occupied by the squirrels unless it had already been taken as a homestead by wild bees; the uppermost hollow, if large enough, was occupied by raccoons, foxes and civit cats.

Much of the training requisite for locating and trailing wild animals to their dens was handed down to the pioneers by some friendly Indians.

The boys were aware that bees are strong drinkers during the hot summer months; they soon learned that bees always drink at the same place, which invariably was at the banks of pools where there was an abundance of drift sand. When such a place was found, with the bees sipping and drinking their fill, excitement ran high. Each boy would fix his eyes on a certain bee and watch it rise high up in the air and fly off in a straight line for its hive. After each boy was sure of the course of the bees, they with,, drew to some shady nook and took up real detective work. The eldest in the crowd would explain that, because the bees scared high up in the air, their hive was more than five hundred yards distant; and since there is another creek in the direction the bees flew, a half mile away, they need not search for the tree beyond one-third of the distance between the two creeks. Often there were such long tendrils of moss hanging about the trunk of the large trees that it made it extremely difficult for them to see the bees' entrance or exit. When all attempts at locating the bee tree within a reasonable time proved futile, a small piece of bee's wax was placed on a bush in an opening between the trees that afforded a good view and a tablespoonful of honey dripped on it which would attract the bees. If then the hive was within a radius of five hundred feet from the food, it was soon located.

As soon as the bee tree was discovered, it was marked, and none save the finder ever dared or ventured to molest or cut down a marked tree irrespective of whose land it was on. Sometimes the boys would cut down the tree after nightfall, when all the bees were in the hive. As soon as the tree crashed to the ground, someone would run up to where the bees had their entrance, stuff a wad of twisted moss into the opening to prevent the bee's escape. That part of the tree occupied by the bees was then hurriedly sawed out, rolled on a slide and hauled to the residence of the finder. The log was then stood on end in some convenient shady place, the wad of moss removed and the bees left unmolested until an empty hive had been procured after which the log was split open, the bees driven into another hive and the honey removed. Some bee trees yielded as much as five gallons of honey, according to their age. Unlike at the present time, honey never ran to sugar during the winter months.

Hogs Fatten on Mast

The pioneer settlers were well supplied with fresh meats each day during the week. Hogs required no particular attention and multiplied rapidly. Each settler had his brand and ear mark recorded at the County seat which enabled him to distinguish and segregate his swine and cattle from those of his neighbors. There being so much mast, grapes, berries, and wild fruit on the ground for the hogs to feed on that the settlers thought it wasteful to feed them corn or swill. The larger portion of hogs came home at night to sleep in the sty made of round logs and a straw roof, while those remaining in the woods turned wild and on spying a hunter would grunt: "hoof, woof" and take to their heels. Just how the hogs managed to build a rain, storm and snow proof nest from leaves and grass, remains an unsolved enigma or problem. They would roll the leaves ana grass with their snout, mould it and place1 it in position as accurately and smoothly as though it had been made of cement reinforced by grass and leaves by a human expert in that line of work.

Wild hogs were considered public property and belonged to the party who succeeded in penning them first. Not infrequently a litter of pigs were caught, ear marked and turned loose again to increase and take care of themselves. Two weeks before slaughtering time, the fattening hogs were penned up, not for the sake of giving them special feed and attention, but to have them at home on the arrival of a cold norther.

Hog killing time was a busy day. The carcasses were strung up high in a tree and left hanging overnight in the air. The next day the carcasses were dismembered and cut up to suit the needs. Exposing the meat to the cold air a certain length of time prior to its manufacture into the finished product made it crisp and tender and more palatable. That is one of the reasons why the sausage of the pioneers made was considered a delicatessen the world over. At the present age, hogs are being slaughtered at nine a.m and converted into sausage at one p.m and given their first smoking at four p.m., which old timers believe accounts for their tough, compressed and hardened condition.

Going a Fishing

The barefoot boy spent much of his leisure time at the creek angling for all sorts of palatable fresh water fish, with which all creeks teemed. Unlike at the present time, fish had developed a splendid appetite and bit like hungry wolves. A scarcity of good bait was always feared by fisherman, although the fish were not the least particular about what was fed them. When the supply of earthworms became exhausted, the hooks were baited with frogs and grasshoppers—a regular pudding for the fish.

Once while the writer was crawling on his hands and knees in search of grasshoppers near the edge of the bank of a creek, he spied the queerest object that his eyes ever beheld. The object appeared as though it had a hundred eyes. I had slipped up to a covey of partridges while they were asleep. Their tails were together; their heads at the outside of the circle. That is the way partridges sleep— sometimes in coveys numbering as many as half a hundred. Aroused by my curiosity, I wanted to know what the object was and hit at it with my slouchy hat. My! there was a flutter of wings that made me feel as though I was in the midst of a whirlwind or in front of a gas well running wild. At another time, I saw a pair of partridges proudly leading a covey of baby birds through the grass at the edge of a fishing pool. Before I got a good glimpse of the roaming birds they were out of sight. Right before me was the mother partridge with a broken wing. I reached out to pick up the wounded bird but it fluttered beyond my reach. I kept following it through the tall grass, all the while thinking of the splendid fish bait she would make but she kept away from me. After I had followed her for some distance, she spread her wings and flew away. Her wing was not broken at all. That is the way partridges protect their brood. She left her baby partridges in the grass and drew me away from them by pretending to be hurt.

In the six years intervening between 1852 and 1859, the following named business enterprises had been established in the old town of New Ulm: Lorenz Mueller, who was the first post master, Robert Wagner, Seehaus, G. Bastian, F. W. Dorbritz, Wangemann Bros., general merchandise, F. Haubold, wheelwright, wagon and broom factory; Mittank, Giebtner, R. Weber, A. Wischnevski and A. Braun, blacksmiths; F. Wolters, saddler; Dohmann, cigar factory; Lueschner, Haemmerlein and Hagemann, breweries; F. Dorbritz and P. Witte, cotton gin; Wangemann Bros., oil mill, located near D. Schweke's cotton gin; G, Mieth, shoemaker; Adolf Peschel, tailor; Christopher Ashorn, tanner; G, Buescher, F, Lingnau and Wm, Moeller, cabinet makers; Wm. Persky, brickyard; R. Rieder, tinner; Dr. A. Hanka, physician and druggist; Rev. R. Roehm, Lutheran minister, residence at Frelsburg.

> *The joys of childhood drift into the pleasures of manhood and young manhood into old age. We hasten on and the clock of time marks the passing hours, but memory pours into our hearts the sweetest melodies, the songs our mother sang pictures again the innocent joys of childhood and we ravel and enjoy the blessings of days gone by. While the pleasures of youth have taken their flight with passing years, we still have the precious boon of memory.*

New Ulm, Texas, Older than New Ulm, Minnesota

Although New Ulm, Texas, and New Ulm, Minnesota, were settled by the same class of immigrants, they knew little of each other until more recently when Athanas Henle, president of the "Junior Pioneers" of New Ulm Minnesota, interested himself in linking the history of the two settlements so widely separated and yet so closely related.

Of the two settlements, New Ulm, Minnesota, is the more prosperous, notwithstanding the fact that a large per cent of the early pioneer settlers fell victims to an Indian massacre and that the pioneers by their own blood sanctified the spot where the beautiful little city of New Ulm, Minnesota, is now located. New Ulm, Minnesota, is beautifully located on a hill side, dotted with numerous monuments, driveways and parks, intermingled with magnificent buildings and busy streets, A. Henle and others whose ancestors paid with their lives for all those beautiful things, are endeavoring to instill in the hearts and minds of the "Junior Pioneers" of their town and county, and rekindle in their souls, the great debt of filial love they owe their forbears, which speaks well for the people of our northern namesake.

The pioneer settlers of New Ulm, Texas, fared much better as regards Indian warfare. The white settlers were seldom molested by the Indians who moved northward when Texas and Mexican armies, commanded by Sam Houston, Santa Anna and other organizations, made their stay unsafe here. The settlers at New Braunfels, Austin and other central Texas settlements did not fare so well as detailed accounts, accessable to those who are interested, show.

The topography of New Ulm, Texas, does not distinguish itself much from the majority of other South Texas towns and of the names of the original settlers, only a few are inscribed on the business roster or carried in the tax rolls of the county. Unfavorable transportation facilities prior to 1892, coupled with the invention and introduction of barbed wire induced many of the descendants of the pioneers to seek their fortune elsewhere and that they made no mistake in seeking a new location is evidenced by the fact that at least a half dozen of them became successful bankers and a still larger per cent became prominent in the business world while others became large landowners. Only a very small per cent returned to their native land.

Approximately twenty thousand acres of land to the east and south of New Ulm is not suited for agriculture and the fact that the land has not increased in value in the past half century accounts for the slow growth and expansion of our splendid little towns. The soil to the north and west of town is admirably adapted to agriculture which is amply supported by the fact that beautiful farm residences dot the highways and byways. Fine breeds of cattle roam about in the pastures, indicative of a prosperous farm life in the country referred to by the traveling public as "the land of milk, wine and honey".

But, notwithstanding, the barrenness of the sandy timbered section adjacent to town, it is possible, but not probable, that New Ulm, Texas, will be numbered among the richest of oil towns in South Texas, within a period of eighteen months. This statement is based on the following facts: a large crew of Torsion Balance men operated here for several weeks, and a certain area covering thousands of acres was immediately mapped off. Oil men from practically every state in the union came in for a block of acreage but only two companies were successful in obtaining acreage. The Abstractor of Austin County and a number of experienced men are working overtime in an effort to get titles straightened out and flaws in the deeds, if any, ironed out. After this, the most important step of all, operations are likely to start. Will the result be a surprise or disappointment? Time alone can tell.

Within the Covers of the Family Album

With the introduction of the round or center table in the homes of the pioneer families, came the family album which occupied a prominent place thereon and was handed visitors immediately upon their taking a reclining position. Whether the album was handed them as a matter of friendship or amusement or pastime, need not detain us since the family album has long since become obsolete.

Alter the disappearance of the family album, the photos were placed on the round or center table, unframed and unprotected. Later, they gave way to the post card container or some other new fangled invention such as phonograph and victrola; but how rarely in all human life a now—yesterday is but lately gone, tomorrow is soon to come—today is nothing—a way station on the road to hope perhaps or a time for memory only and for tears. We appreciate the things most when they are no longer in sight, when beyond our reach and when taken away from us through the hand of fate or poor judgment. In our youth, we inadvertently shove things down the steep abyss of oblivion as a result of our narrow mindedness and nearsightedness, and to endeavor to recover them when the snow of winter begins to settle upon our brows.

How rich the heart of even-time that has its garners full. How dear, at that still time of day, the magic of old memories, the breath of violets, the perfume of the honey-suckle, the sight of the broad sloping hillsides covered with a thick mantel of blue-bonnets in early spring—the fragrance cf hay new-mown under the summer sun—the incense of burning cedar set into flame by Christmas candles!

How soft, is the glow of firelight on long gone winter nights; how easily unloosed the strings that binds the letters of an unforgotten youth; how fair the pictured faces of boys and girls we knew when we were young!

Surely it was a poet and a lover of dreams who first thought of making a photograph album and doubly dear among the treasures brought into being by his love, those ornate and portly old albums within whose padded covers and behind whose big brass clasps are kept the modest cartes de visite which were the fashionable photographs during the pioneer days and the years that closely followed them. Rarely among all the things we may possess, do we find a treasure trove more full of memory and love than one of these. It serves as an index to the book of generations and offers us the key that unlocks the possibilities of life. It recalls to us the memory of our childhood days, the old log cabin residence surrounded by a stake and rider zigzag rail fence. Here are the faces our mothers and grandmothers loved, fragile records of five generations in Texas, whose beauty of living and whose heroisms told to us at our fathers knees once filled our childhood fancies with wonder and with pride. Always in these old albums is a picture of somebody's mother, gentle and dignified; far too frail for hard work, yet the one whose slender shoulders bore the heaviest burdens during her earthly career in (he "land of the free and the home of the brave". And then the young girls; frivolous things after the eternal fashion of their kind, wearing strange looking hats, tilted to impossible angles, letting their fancies run to curious coiffures and allowing their steps to be hampered by cumbersome skirts in a way to which no independent young person of today would for an instant submit, except at a masquerade ball. These were the girls whose loveliness was so tantalizing, whose sweetness was so spirited, and whose loyalty was so dauntless and unafraid. Such pictures are time-yellowed now and just a little dim. Measured by the actual years since they were made, they are not very old, but to us now, across the gaping chasm of the world's new wounds, they belong, to a day that might seem infinitely remote did we not know that it was infinitely vital still in the undying spirit that it has bequested to us.

We smile at the fading faces tenderly, recalling old faiths old braveries and old loves, and our eyes are wet and our hearts are big with pride when we remember that back of the courage and the fearless sacrifice of our young crusaders of the war just done, stand the deathless traditions of honor and loyalty and love of God that were the breath of life to these men and women passed now forever from our sight except for a handful of time-dimmed pictures shut within the covers of an old album.

Perhaps the new "younger generation", which looks upon the old regime as a legendary part, will smile tolerantly upon those' fading faces, lent to those who remember with sympathetic understanding, they will resurrect from the deep still chambers of the heart "spectus dim" of the old life of which they were a part, doubly appealing now that it belongs to history.

Alvin Haubold

The subject of this sketch was born in the old town of New Ulm more than three score and ten years ago. His father, F. Haubold, was the first blacksmith, wheelwright and social leader of New Ulm prior and immediately following the civil war. Alvin learned his father's trade and worked therein until his removal to the railway station in 1893, engaging in the saloon business in the building now occupied by the Cooperative Store. During the years following the invasion of the boll weevil into this section, business was less remunerative causing many to bid farewell to the town of their birth. Among them was A. Haubold who located at Waco. That he is still interested in his native town is evidenced by the fact that he contributed his mite making the publication of this manual possible.

C. A. Dorbritz

Another scion of an old time pioneer family is C. A, Dorbritz. "A tinner by profession and a postmaster by birth" is the title given him by his friends and acquaintances of a lifetime. Born in the old town of New Ulm prior to declaration of war between the states, he attended the local schools and in addition received special business training in his father's store, wherein he worked as clerk and assistant postmaster. After the death of his father, F. W. Dorbritz, he received the appointment for the postmastership and held the position until the new town was established.

C. A. Dorbritz, Son of a pioneer family.

During the official administrations of Gus. Voigt, M. W. Krueger, E. A, Schulze and Louis O. Muenzler he has been serving as assistant postmaster giving excellent satisfaction to the postoffice patrons. In speaking of his efficiency as a public servant his friends venture to say that he needs no deck or time-piece guiding him in the opening or closing of official business.

Cat Spring

Although approximately only 16 miles apart the business relations between New Ulm and Cat Spring are few and far between, notwithstanding the fact that during the pioneering of Austin County the inhabitants had much in common and worked harmoniously for the betterment of their future welfare. The deep sand that separates the two neighboring towns on the Katy makes motor traffic exceedingly tedious and, in the event of car trouble, unhandy because of the sparsely settled timberland, which, in the event of a break down, would necessitate many miles of travel through deep sand before reaching a farmhouse where help might be expected.

Among the first German settlers who located at Cat Spring were Carl and Marcus Amsler, who later erected the first dance hall at that place. Next came the Rudolf von Roeder family, consisting of father, mother, six sons and four daughters. Mr. Roeder received a league of land as a reward for his assistance in getting other grants surveyed. One of Mr. Roeder's sons shot and killed a Mexican puma on the Glsor farm situated opposite the farm now owned by Arthur C. Stuessel. The puma had come to the spring to drink when spied by the successful hunter, hence the name of the town.

Christian Amthor, a pioneer settler of Cat Spring, was chosen first county surveyor of Austin

County. Mr. Amthor, a kind and generous man, did much in encouraging settlers to locate at Cat Spring and was a true friend to the new home seekers.

The first agricultural society in the state was organized at Cat Spring many, many years ago. The handwriting on the stationery used by the club officials, immediately following the civil wat, is the finest on record, which shows what it shows.

On numerous recent visits to Cat Spring and vicinity the author had ample opportunity to convince himself of the longevity of the pioneer settlers. Mrs. A. Brast, who resides with her son near the Colorado County line, is still hale and hearty at the age of 103 years. Others had reached the serene old age of 95 years when they fell asleep in the arms of Jesus.

Mrs. C. Ladig, although now in her 85th year is as spry and active as a person of 50 and is as handy with the saw and hammer as a middle aged carpenter.

New Bremen

New Bremen, formerly known as Kuykendall, is a flourishing settlement in the timber belt northeast of New Ulm. Abner Kuykendall, Renkip Stoeltje, Mat and Henriette Steussy, Robert Harvey, John Breeding and Rudolf Von Roeder were among the first to receive grants of land and located there prior to the out break of the civil war.

About the year 1846, A. D. Heitmann and his young bride of a few months settled in the Stoeltje (originally Abner Kuykendall) survey and soon thereafter other settlers were attracted which resulted in the carving of a beautiful settlement out of the timberland and the virgin soil of the open flats or prairies. Heitmann attained a serene old age of four score and ten years and even at that age rode horseback to Cat Spring and Industry on Saturdays. Other old time settlers were: Fritz and George Luedke, F, W. Hackbarth, Ed. Brune, Wm, Saage, George Berger, Carl Lesikar, Wm. Dierke, Albert Jacobi, Ludwig Hoppe, Ludwig Wienke, Frank and Joe Lala, Meissner, Andreas, Fischer, Itosder, Findeisen, Gebert, Kirsche, Janecek, Springborn, Hohle, Blazinger, Hinkel, Fila, Domesle, Franke, Lockwood and others.

With the introduction of motor vehicles a demand for better, more constructive and more convenient dirt roads arose which resulted in the building of several straight roads to New Ulm, Industry and Nelsonville. Said dirt roads run lengthwise and crosswise through that once isolated and cutoff section which now enables farmers to carry their products to market with ease and rapidity. The landowners gave freely of their time and money for the building of dirt roads, well knowing that a network of good passable roads enhances the value of real estate.

In the recent past the commissioner's court established New Bremen a voting precinct. The inhabitants are progressively inclined which is evidenced by the fact that they were among the first to vote upon themselves a legitimate local school tax for the maintenance of their school.

Frelsburg

The pioneers who carved Frelsburg out of an untamed wilderness were closely associated with those of New Ulm, Industry and Cat Spring, inasmuch as their hardships and privations prior to the cessation of hostilities between the states were practically the same.

Wm. Frels, Pieper, Yordt, Zimmerscheidt, Leyendecker and others made history for that particular settlement during the pioneer days and unconsciously perpetuated their names in the annals of Colorado County, Texas. Messrs Frels and Pieper were given much publicity by historians and press correspondents and well deserve the approbations lavishly bestowed upon them in recognition of their courageous adventures and success in carving a flourishing settlement out of a wilderness. D. F. F. Yordt, who came here prior to Texas being a state led a very adventurous life. From the only files available we gather that Mr. Yordt arrived here about the year 1837, with no particular destination in view. His young wife and two sons remained in Germany awaiting his return to the fatherland from the land of plenty unlimited opportunities. Although past middle age Yordt enlisted in the Confederate army as a private but was soon promoted to the ranks of a captain and otherwise distinguished himself because of his superior training in the land of his birth.

After receiving his discharge he returned to his

family in his native land. In the meantime, however, Yordt had grown up in age and could not persuade his wife to return with him to Texas. Finally she gave her consent for her two sons to accompany their father to the broad expanse of Texas. One of the sons, according to old files, was appointed postmaster at Frelsburg and also conducted a mercantile business there for many years. We have no way of knowing the whereabouts of their posterity, if any they had.

Shortly after the close of the civil war Frelsburg had the distinction of being a business town of considerable prominence, despite its isolated location and long distance from a railroad station. Kollmann, Pophanken, Duerr, Heinrichs, Kohlloeffel and perhaps others did a thriving business there in the days of long ago.

.The people of Frelsburg and surrounding territory were highly patriotic and loyal to their government which is best evidenced by the fact that a league of land was granted them through the efforts of Sam Houston, governor of Texas, as a small token of appreciation for their valiant services in the wars with Mexico. This grant of land was intended to furnish means for the education of their children. For more than a quarter of a century the Herman seminary served a noble purpose in the educational line. The original building, a two story structure, was destroyed by fire in 1926, but has since been replaced by a commodious three-teacher school building.

The town has two magnificent church buildings, two mercantile establishments, a cotton gin, blacksmith shop and dance hall. Most of the inhabitants of Frelsburg and its trades territory patronize the New Ulm State Bank of which financial institution one of their townsmen, Robert Heinsohn, is a director.

Charles Leyendecker, a descendant of an influential pioneer family is still hale and hearty and physically able to manage his farm with remarkable success. F. L. Brune, H. Schuette and August Becker are among the oldest living people in the community. F. G. Kollmann, Geo. Herder, Christian, John and Henry Paasch, Weishuhn, Breudigan, Vogelsang, Ordner, Westphal, Ramthum and others are descendant of pioneer families.

Rev. J. C. Roehm.

In furnishing the readers with a brief sketch of the difficulties experienced by Rev. J. C. Roehm in organizing the Lutheran church congregation at Frelsburg, in 1852 we can do nothing better than translate from manuscript in German furnished us by Rev. O. Lindenberg, Lutheran minister of New Ulm and Frelsburg, the follow along excerpts from Rev. Roehm's own notations:

"Leaving La Grange on my way to Ross Prairie, where 1 intended organizing a Lutheran church congregation, I encountered various obstacles which seemed almost insurmountable. I had previously collected names and addresses of families I desired to consult and started out to befriend them. The first family I accosted was unable to provide for me for lack of accommodations at their disposal. My stop at the second family residence was brief and less courteous, more so perhaps, because of my unexpected appearance. Not losing courage I continued my trip to the residence of a family residing about six miles distant, on the romantic banks of Cumings Creek.

Friendly and courteous settlers directed me from one farm to the other until I arrived at Mr. and Mrs. K's residence, where the noon meal was just being served. The savory milk-rice pudding sharpened my appetite almost beyond control but all in vain—I was not invited to eat at their table and my pride forbade that I become intrusive. The family disregarded my presence and had no pity on me, although I was very hungry and cold. On presenting my card the head of the family directed me to the home of his brother, one mile distant, where I arrived at one o'clock tired and footsore. After relating my experiences, and telling of the unwelcome reception given me at the residences I had stopped, I was welcomed and bid to make myself comfortable and consider his residence as my temporary home. I felt much relieved and thankful for having at last found a convenient place to eat and sleep. My mission was to visit as many settlers of my faith as possible within a radius of twelve miles and encourage them to worship with us at the home of Mr. and Mrs. K. This required approximately two weeks, however, considering existing conditions, I felt gratified because of my success."

Frelsburg

Rev. Roehm offered to pastorate the congregation for a period of six months hoping in the meantime to find suitable quarters for himself and family. For his services he was promised a purse of $43. For a while all went well and the church services, in private residences were well attended. Later an effort was made to erect a parsonage providing sufficient room for church services and for housing a parochial school. The erection of a log house with a commodious back room was taken under advisement. Mr. K. offered to furnish all the required logs and lumber requisite for the building 20 x 24 feet, gratis. An animated discussion followed wherein all delegates participated. The location of the new edifice was a difficult matter to decide. Some few favored a central location while others wanted the house of worship as near their home as possible. Those residing several miles north of Frelsburg insisted tenaciously that the church be built in the town of Frelsburg, where a number of residences, a store, a blacksmith shop and a post office already existed and where a Catholic church had already been built.

One of the delegates exclaimed "We are not going with you down into the timberland" "and we are not going with you up into the prairie" another delegate shot back at him. Another faction arose exclaiming: "If you are not going south with us, we are not going north with you." Consequently the meeting was adjourned without reaching a definite decision.

Because of the absence of suitable quarters wherein to hold church services and teaching school a private residence, located in the prairie was chosen as a substitute, however, the attendance was so discouraging that the holding of divine services was no longer justified. Rev. Roehm exclaimed "My efforts are in vain." Immediately thereafter Rev. Roehm received a call from the Lutheran church at Galveston, He accepted but still returned to Frelsburg to attend to his ministerial duties off and on.

On June 5, 1855, the Lutheran church at Frelsburg was organized with the following named parties appointed as spiritual court: Rev. J. C: Roehm, J. Krause, G. Fehrenkamp, R. Stoeltje and L. Kaiser. The following members constituted the first congregation: George Kaiser, F. Hillmer, John Kaiser, H. Voskamp, F. Frerichs, Gerhard Mehrens, H. Hillmann, L. Hillmann, S. Struss, Gottlieb Volmar, J. H. Koepke, C. Aschenbeck, C. Linke, John Schultz, Theo. Becker, W. Frerichs, J. F. Stolle, J. Guthmann, and H. Schmiedekamp.

Captain Wm. Freis donated 3.9 acres of land for church, school, parsonage and cemetery purposes.

Later when Rev. Roehm discontinued his visits to Frelsburg Rev. F. Gerstmann took charge of the congregation and remained on his post of duty for more than a quarter of a century.

Mr. A. Mathias, a resident of Boggy Branch, was the first organist of the Lutheran church and was employed at a salary of $25 per annum.

In 1879 Prof. C. Klaerner took charge of the parochial school at a salary of $450.00 per term.

Prof. Klaerner also relieved Mr. Mathias as organist.

Rev. Roehm's name was a household word among the pioneer settlers of this section because of his fine traits of character, coupled with his undaunted courage and cheerful, sunny disposition. He died at a serene old age in his home in the "Island City" highly beloved and honored by his friends of a lifetime.

On October 15, 1930, the Lutheran church at Frelsburg celebrated its diamond jubilee.

New Ulm A Railroad Town

When the Missouri, Kansas and Texas, engine blew its first steam whistle at the present townsite of New Ulm, in 1892, great excitement prevailed. There was a scramble for business and residential lots inducing many farmers to invest in town property. The buzz of saw and hammer took the place of the barking of the squirrels, the hooting of the owl and the squawk of the crow. The old shacks in the old town were torn down and the usable lumber used in the erection of new buildings at the railway station. Five years later the town numbered 225 inhabitants. The business section comprised five general merchandise stores, two furniture stores, six saloons, a saddlery and harness shop, two blacksmiths, two tins hops, two cotton platforms, two livery stables, two lumberyards, a soda water factory, one barber, and a wholesale brewery agency. There were 75 children enumerated in the school district. In 1898, 7,627 bales of cotton were shipped from the local station and in 1899 the number of bales had increased to 8,398. During the same period 4,739 crates of eggs, 1,528 coops of poultry and 128 buckets of butter were shipped from here to the wholesale markets. The gross receipts for freight and passenger fares amounted to $25,537.18 during the same year.

The gross receipts at the local railway station for the year 1929 amounted to $54,000. This large increase is due to the large carload shipments of pipes for the laying of two pipelines through territory adjacent to New Ulm. The shipments of poultry and eggs is practically the same as formerly despite the fact that fully seventy percent of that class of freight is being transported to the wholesale markets by trucks and cars. Fewer than 150 bales of cotton were shipped from this station during 1929 because of the truck competition. According to an estimate furnished us from a reliable source 8,000 bales of cotton within New Ulm's trades territory are being withheld from the market by farmers and speculators.

About the year 1900 came a lull in the business line because of a series of short crops and a depression in the market value of farm products which prompted the business men and farmers to organize a creamery which was a success at the beginning but not in the long run. The smaller shareholders were absorbed by the larger ones which accounts for its ultimately closing down.

In 1898, when New Ulm numbered only 225 inhabitants Mr. Yates founded the "New Ulm News" which soon became dormant and prompted Mr. Yates to seek greener fields. In 1910, John B. Moran established the "New Ulm Enterprise" and for six months published a daily paper here with remarkable success. After the withdrawal of Mr. Moran from the publication it changed hands numerous times until 1919 when Louis O. Muenzler acquired same by purchase and conducted its management until his appointment to the postmastership of New Ulm in 1929, when his oldest son Harry was automatically promoted to the ranks of publisher and general manager.

At present New Ulm's business roster is composed as follows: five general stores, one department store, one hardware store, two undertakers, five soda water dispensaries, three restaurants, one hotel, two daily meat markets, two barber shops, one tailor, two garages, four filling stations, one lumberyard, one soda water factory, one state bank, one newspaper, one radio agency, one physician, two visiting dentists, two patent medicine salesmen, one gin and grist mill, one miniature oil mill, one blacksmith shop, two carpenters, a high school, a lutheran church three rural mail carriers. Population: 500.

The German Element

It is not in a spirit of boasting, but with a pardonable pride in the important part of the people of German extraction have had in the development of our county and state at large that this chapter is being written. From the earliest times the German element played its active part in the development of Texas, the same as in many other states of the union.

The German pioneers who settled in this section of the state prior to 1860, were a hardy stock of people and were not of the floating type who would return to their former home either after striking it rich, or after meeting with disappointment in the land of their adoption; but they at once became permanent citizens who by their toil and thrift helped to build a state of which they and their posterity may justly be proud. With but a very few exceptions they took an active interest in all civic and political affairs, which is best substantiated by the fact that many of them hold positions of trust and honor and performed their duties faithfully and efficiently, as ever thereafter.

In the wars of the United States the Germans always took an honorable part, thereby giving evidence of their loyalty to their state and nation of which their rude log cabin dwelling house in the land of their adoption is a component part. Those who had renounced allegiance to the government of the land of their birth in order to pledge fealty to the land of their adoption, were just as eager to defend their new home, whenever the need arose, than were their sons who were born under the stars and stripes and had never seen the land of their fathers.

When the civil war broke out great numbers of Germans enlisted as volunteers in the Confederate army in defense of their beloved South. During the World War, which truly was the crucial test of the German-Americans' patriotism and loyalty to the land of their choice, we find the sam« spirit of true service to their country prevailing among them as in former wars of our country. In untold numbers they willingly offered their services in the hour of need, which in many instances even compelled them to oppose their own blood-relations on the field of battle. No greater proof of loyalty than this can be given, nor rightfully asked, than that which has been given by the people of German descent in Texas and the nation at large during the supreme crises.

The German language which for so long a time had been taught in the elementary and high schools of Texas, has been grossly neglected, not to say excluded or barred from the school curriculum because of the narrow mindedness of those not familiar with that cultural language. For two hundred fifty years German has been an American language second only to the English. The German singing societies and "Turnvereins" have even with the use of the German language wielded an enormous influence for good upon the American Citizenship and family life. If German is spoken in German-clubs and society circles, it does not mean that English is not understood and used there, so that the Germans are in a position to be their own interpreters to the English-speaking public as to their aims and purposes. But at the same time they can preserve unto themselves and their fellow citizens the many desirable features of their own time-tested traditions, which would not be possible were the German language recklessly discarded to be arbitrarily supplanted by the English.

Among the German language newspapers most closely identified with the people of Austin County, is "Das Wochenblatt" (now published at the state capitol) which began its useful and colorful career at Bellville, about 1890, from which time it has been published without interruption to this day. It successfully weathered the stormy years of the World War, surviving a crises which was the death of many similar publications throughout the length and breadth of the country, a fact which speaks well for the loyal American spirit of the publisher and readers of "Das Wochenblatt."

Beginnings of New Ulm, Minnesota

and Community Related, Together with Personal Experiences

By Athanas Henle[5]

In giving a true history of what our parents suf-

---

[5] Athanasius Henle 6 December 1829 - 22 October 1893. He came to America when he was quite young and was one of the original settlers of the New Ulm, Minnesota area. (Athanasius Henle, Ludwig Meyer, Frank Massopust and Alois Plamer were the 4 men who selected the present site of New Ulm for the town site on October 7, 1854).
In 1856 he married Elizabeth Fink, traveling by an ox team to get married by a Catholic priest in St. Paul, Minnesota. It is said that 24 of the Henle relatives/family lost their lives in the Sioux Uprising of 1862, including Athanasius's wife Elizabeth's parents John & Monika Fink and Elizabeth's brother Max. In 1893 Athanasisus & Elizabeth moved to New Ulm from Milford and he died on the same year on October 22, 1893.
Of the twelve children he had with his wife Elizabeth, only 6 were alive at the time of his death.
His obituary stated that "some of his ways were distinctly peculiar to him, he was respected by all his acquaintances and fellow citizens".
(https://www.findagrave.com/memorial/37521711/athanasius-henle)

fered in opening this section to civilization, we feel that every citizen, whether he settled here in the early days, or only last year, will participate in the concerted endeavor to honor the memory of the founders of our city, in recognition of the rich blessings which we now enjoy as a result of their labors.

It was in the year 1852, when a group of sturdy young men and women of Erbach[6], Wuerttenberg, became seriously interested in a plan to devote their future life to aiding in the development of the New World, as they called America. This plan materialized, and in the same year, a party of these young people emigrated from their native soil, and landed in New York City.

Not finding that city to their liking as a future home, the party came West, and located in Chicago, Ill., for some time. During their leisure hours, the young people took instruction in the English language, meanwhile formulating various plans seeking to find a suitable place for their proposed settlement.

In the year 1853, there appeared in the Illinois Staatszeitung of Chicago, a call for the first meeting of this brave little group and their friends. The object was to form an association, which was to foster the settlement project. After a few subsequent meetings, the membership had increased to

---

6 Erbach an der Donau is a town on the Danube River in Baden-Württemberg, Germany. Located in the Alb-Donau District, Erbach lies between Ulm and Ehingen an der Donau on the southern edge of the Swabian Jura.

50. "Deutscher Landverein" (German Land Society) was the name chosen, and monthly dues were fixed at 10 cents per member.

Realizing that they would not be able to raise money fast enough with only the small monthly dues, two dances were arranged, which netted $300.

The membership increased rapidly, and soon 300 were enrolled, which, in a few months, jumped to 800. That there was much discussion, and many plans offered, naturally hardly needs to be mentioned. Finally, two men—Messrs. Weiss and Kiesling—went west, and, upon their return, reported of the beautiful scenery of Minnesota, whereupon the colony decided to come to this state.

Athanas Henle New Ulm, Minnesota

But, when it came to face the proposition

squarely, only a very small number of the members enlisted to strike out and seek a suitable location for their settlement. We believe it noteworthy to give the names of the courageous men and women who comprised that sturdy little group and joined the colony. They are: M. Wall, M. Walser, Athanas and Anton Henle, Joseph Dambach, Jacob David, and Leonard Haeberle, Ludwig Meyer and two sons, W. Winkelmann, Alois Palmer, J, Klinkhammer, John and Peter Mack, Mr. and Mrs. Cassimir Hermann, Kraemer, Joseph Schwarz, Weiss, Elizabeth Fink, (who later became the wife of Athanas Henle),Mr. and Mrs F. Julius and one child, Voehringer, Wiedenmann, Frank Massopust, K, Kleinknecht, Mr. and Mrs. J. Zettel and one child, William Thiele, J. Brandt, J. Keck, and Benedict Drexler. (The, six last named were killed by the Sioux during the massacre in 1862).

The trip from Chicago to their destination, about 600 miles, was partly traveled by rail, and the balance by the Minnesota river steamboat, "Jeanette Robertos", as far as Travus D. Siouse.

The names of Le Sueur and Swan lake having been mentioned to the travelers, they decided to make thorough investigations, desiring to locate at the most favorable place. To accomplish this, 11 men left the company and struck out as scouts. After tramping through tall grass for a day, seven men lost courage and returned, while the four others—Athanas Henle, Ludwig Meyer. Frank Massopust, and Alois Palmer—continued the tedious journey. They walked all the way from

Travers D. Sious, where they left the colony, past Swan lake, as far as Fort Ridgely, where they saw a house.

Going up to the house at midnight, the weary travelers rapped on the door. Someone inside called out, in French, "Who is there?" After Mr. Palmer had answered for his party, they were welcomed by the frenchman La Framboise, who lived there. The men had traveled for two days with but very little food, and greatly appreciated the generous hospitality of their host, who prepared supper for them. Mr. La Framboise, who had married an Indian squaw, asked his guests if they knew what kind of meat they were eating. "Jack rabbits," was the ready response, but the Frenchman called it muskrat meat.

On their expedition, the four men, in the month of October, had to sleep under a tree, with nothing but scant clothing to protect themselves from the chilly night air.

Mr. La Framboise proved himself very generous to those pioneer scouts. He told them about the beautiful site where two rivers flow together, and personally accompanied them, to make certain that they would not go the wrong way. The Frenchman deserves much credit for his efforts in assisting the colony to settle here.

Joyfully, the four men returned and reported about the picturesque location which they had found. To make sure that no one else would locate there, the party had taken a long stick, tied grass around the top of it, and placed it on the site, indicating that it had been taken. On their way back to the colonists, they met a few covered wagons. The scouts became aroused, fearing they might now lose the spot, selected by them. However, upon inquiring, they learned that the travelers were a party of government surveyors.

The colonists arrived here, October 7, 1854, (the date which the Junior Pioneers now observe annually with a very successful banquet). It being late in the fall, the question naturally arose, where to find shelter for the winter? The Indians, who, until a short time before, had owned the land, left three tepees behind, when they departed, and in these deserted tepees the settlers took shelter during the winter. However, some of the red men had been afflicted with smallpox, while living in these tepees, and several members of the colony contracted the disease. Fortunately, however, no one died.

In the spring, when the Indians returned and found their tepees occupied by the "palefaces",1 they became very much aroused. Through the intercession of La Framboise, the settlers were placed on friendly terms with the Indians, and no Sioux would ever have molested a man, woman, or child, had the government agents treated them as ordered by the government.

Our young generation may be interested to learn where the early white settlers moved to, after spending the winter in the Indian tepees. Don't think for a moment, dear children, that there was a seven-room brick house, with heating, electric lights, gas, telephone, radio, etc., waiting for them to move in. While the colonists lived in the primitive Indian lodgings, the men started to build log houses. They felled large trees, hewed them on both sides and fitted them at the corners. Boards for the roof were sawed from logs by means of hand saws; the rafters were split from straight-grained trees, and shingles were split from blocks and whittled into shape. In many instances, long slough grass was used to thatch the roofs. The cornice, made of undried boards, in time shrunk, giving ample space for drifting snow to enter the house, and many a young pioneer will recall, that, after a snowstorm, they were covered with snow, in bed. A detailed account of what the pioneers and their children experienced, would prove interesting, as compared with the great advancement made during the subsequent years.

Coming back to the colony which settled eight miles west of New Ulm. They were divided on the matter of a townsite. A powerful stream of water, later known as Vajen's creek, in the town of Milford was favorably considered as a possible source of waterpower, and the heavy growth of timber also was a strong factor. Some numbers of the colony proposed to establish a townsite on what is now the Henry P. Bastian farm in that township, but a majority preferred the present townsite of New Ulm, and their choice prevailed. Most of the first settlers having come from Ulm Württemberg, they decided on "New Ulm" as the name for their colony here.

In 1856, a group of people arrived in this city from Cincinnati, Ohio, and by mutual consent, the two colonies merged, under the name of German Land Association of Minnesota. Additional settlers arrived, as time went on, and soon stores, houses, and shops sprung up in the new settlement, which flourished beautifully.

In looking over the records of New Ulm's pioneer days, I find that the women, who experienced the severest hardships during the Indian uprising, were not given adequate consideration. These women were my mother, Elizabeth Henle, and Mrs. Florian Hartmann, later Mrs. John Bobleter.

Miss Elizabeth Fink, who was a maid in a castle at Erbach, Wuerttenberg, Germany, joined a party of emigrants in 1852 to make America her future home. Among these emigrants was Athanas Henle to whom she was married in 1856, as records show. They drove to St. Paul with an ox team to get married by a Catholic priest.

The Fink family, composed of John, Martin and Monika Fink, the parents, Elizabeth and two married sisters, Barbara Zettel and Lucretia Zeller and their families, settled in Milford township where they lived happily, though frugally, until August 18, 1862. On Aug. 18, 1862, mother's parents and the families of her sisters were killed. Those who were killed were John Martin Fink and his wife Monika. Max Fink, their son; Carl Merkle, their grandson; Florian Hartmann; John Baptist Zettel and his wife Barbara Zettel, and their children, Elizabeth, Stephan, Anton and Johanna; Max Zeller and his wife, Lucretia Zeller, and their children John, Monika, Cecelia, Conrad and Martin; Anton Messmer and his wife Mary

Anna Messmer and their son, Joseph; and Martin Anton and Mary, Children of Anton Henle.

Joy Riding in Minnesota

Our parents were very kind to the Indians. One old Indian appreciated this so much, that several days before the uprising, he warned mother with the words, "Pokatschi," which means to leave home, and "Nippo" which means killing. Father was not at home, and mother paid no attention to the faithful Indian's warning. Near noon on August 18th our horse, "Katie" came home, which she never did before. My parents were very much surprised in having her come home at that unusual time, but "Katie" seemed to feel what was coming. Being busy stacking their small amount of grain they tied her to a tree and continued with their work. A few minutes later they heard shooting. While they were still wondering what this meant, our nearest neighbor, Casimer Hermann, who lived about forty rods west also near the timber, came running and shouting, "Athanas, come as quickly as you can, the Indians are killing everybody they meet."

Our parents left their work at once and called us four children. Father took sister Crescenzia and myself under his arm, and mother took Mary and Martin, then jumped on the horse and made it go as fast as it could travel toward the ferry on the Minnesota, river which was about 160 rods from our home.

After having arrived at the ferry, father requested Alois Palmer, the owner of the ferry to take us over as quickly as possibly, Mr. Palmer wanted to get his gun and money first but father and Mr. Hermann, realizing that delay was dangerous, decided to ferry us across the river. We had hardly reached the other side and hidden in the bushes when the Indians appeared on the shore. While father was searching for a wagon to which our horse might be hitched to take us to New Ulm, the Indians passed us at close range. Mother was nearly overcome by worry on account of father, because she thought he had now surely fallen into the hands of the Indians.

When the Indians had killed everyone they could in this settlement, they crossed the Minnesota river and made their way toward Fort Ridgeley. When father saw the Indians coming, he hid in the brush and then returned to us with a wagon which he had found. Our horse was hitched to the wagon, and we set out toward New Ulm. On the way father warned all the people who lived in close range; and by the time we reached New Ulm, there were thirty-seven women and children piled into that wagon. At New Ulm we were all placed in the Erd's building where Wd. Eibneer's confectionery store is at present located. This spot is now marked with a tableau.

Father obtained a rifle from a little Irishman who was half scared to death, and with this rifle stood guard day and night without sleep.

Fourteen days after the battle Athanas and Anton Henle, Mack and Palmer decided to go back to their farms and see what was left of them. When they were about eight miles west of New Ulm, they noticed what they thought to be a squaw, and one of the men aimed at her, but father pulled down the gun and said that four men ought to be able to handle one Indian squaw.

The supposed squaw mistook the men for Indians, and hid among the corn, crawling between the rows toward the timber to her hiding place. This woman was Mrs. Florian Hartman, whose husband had been shot, and she saved her life by hiding in a hole which the animals had made in a ravine. Mrs. Hartman had spent fourteen days and nights in this dugout, nourishing herself like the birds. The dog had followed her, and as he barked continuously, she strangled him with her apron strings to avoid detection by the Indians.

One night, when all was quiet, she decided to go to her house, which had not been burned by the redskins, for food. As she entered the house she noticed an Indian moving in her bed. Blood stains in the bed indicated that he was wounded. She fled at once but he had seen her and sent several bullets after her which luckily missed their mark. When the other settlers returned, she had already returned to her home and was working the homestead. While at work she saw Indians pass who retreated from the battle at New Ulm. Not seeing any white people for seventeen days, she cried out many times, "My God, am I left alone in this world."

Mrs. Hartman was the sister of Athanas and Anton Henle. She later married John Bobleter and spent her declining years in a small frame house in New Ulm.

When I recall the early days in which our parents suffered the loss of relatives and friends besides all their earthly goods, I fully realize now why mother often shed tears. She was many times asked to relate her early experiences, but she never liked to talk about them. Nearly 40 relatives made the supreme sacrifice.

Big Trees from Little Acorns Grow

Practically all of New Ulm's business men were reared on a farm in the backwoods. During their boyhood days they helped their fathers pick cotton, cut corn tops, pull corn, rope off the calves and slop the pigs. Walking barefooted in the fresh plow furrow behind a yoke of oxen or a pair of reliable horses was their chief delight. On Sundays the boys of the neighborhood went a-fishing, nutting, if it happened to be late in the fall. The woods were full of huckleberries, black haws, red haws, persimmons, winter grapes and other varieties of wild fruit familiar to the old timers. In winter they walked to the one teacher school barefooted often nursing a sore toe or two which they had neatly bandaged and incased in a wrapper made of bleached domestic soaked in turpentine, and tied on with a piece of sewing thread to prevent its slipping off. In the fall of the year instead of hearing their elders discuss and argue the possible mileage they could get out of a gallon of gas, they heard them express their eagerness to liquidate their charge account. One of the main topics of conversation among visitors on Sundays was the liquidations of their indebtedness to their respective creditor. Visitors were allowed to take a squint into the pantry, notably into the flour barrel and meal sack, and occasionally would lift the oil can to estimate the supply of oil on hand. The price of groceries or drygoods was seldom discussed—they got more pleasure estimating the size of the crop to be harvested and the probable revenue they expected to derive therefrom. The planting and cultivation of one acre of land to cotton was equivalent to the harvesting of one bale under ordinary weather condition. Often farmers were unable to gather all of their cotton crop, and when that happened they permitted others to pick it on halves. The seed was left at the gins forasmuch as the commercial value as a fertilizer or some other byproduct had not yet been discovered.

Sweet potatoes grew so prolific that it was not uncommon for the tubers to protrude from the ground to the gratification of stock cattle. However, heavy spring rains year after year washed and leached the soil to such an extend that crab grass, which grows rank on the thinnest soil, made farming a burden. Then, too, the sudden appearance of the jack rabbit and the mole or gopher, made the growing of sweet potatoes unprofitable in localities where they once grew without cultivation. The big heavy corn ears of which one hundred in number would usually fill a flour barrel ceased to attain their former size and gradually made nubbins of which it required two hundred to fill a barrel. Cotton, too, lost much of its former prestige and failed to yield as readily as formerly. Diversification and intensive farming was just in its experimental stage and as there was not sufficient barn yard fertilizer to spread over more than twenty percent of the cultivated land; soil refertilization was slow and tedious. Under such prevailing conditions the young men were eager to leave the farm and secure employment with some mercantile firm in order to familiarize themselves with merchandizing inasmuch as little capital was required to run a store—the wholesalers were very liberal in extending credit to the merchants.

All went well until about the year 1890 when the tide turned against the credit system, which in the meantime became habitual, not to say a nuisance, and threatened to ruin the commercial world. The attitude of the consuming public started an aggressive movement against the producers, or vice verse, which caused considerable friction between buyer and seller. The manufacturer advocated the reduction of the cotton acreage while the cotton growers advocated the lengthening of the shirt tail six inches in order to equalize consumption and production. Since then a great change has taken place. The small two room farm dwellings have been replaced by substantial residences, the old barns are gone and new ones erected instead, the raising of poultry and dairy cattle is giving employment to those who formerly got much pleasure out of fishing and hunting, and the toot of the auto horn has taken the place of the ox-whip. School children ride to school in elegant motor cars, farmers ride to the cotton fields in their new model family car with a slide tied on to the rear axle on which they drag their cotton home noon and night. The merchants all over the country are compelled to stock their shelves with the rarest and most costly silks in order to accommodate their customers with the choicest piece goods that money can buy. Groceries are no longer sold in bulk as formerly. Everything comes in cartons or wrappers. Gas is being retailed through rubber hose, canned music is being furnished by Radio and Phonographs and rural people have their mail box at the front gate. The telephone is another invention calculated to bring city service to the rural people. But in spite of all New Ulm's business men faced the problems of the commercial world nobly and manly irrespective of the heavy losses sustained through bad debts, slow collections and loss of property through thefts perpetrated by professional burglars.

During the World War the business world held the sack open for them which enabled the farsighted ones to lay up some fuel for the future. Cotton sold at 42 cents per pound, seed at $80 per ton and other commodities in proportion. A new mode of living started. Much time was spent dancing, rejoicing and frolicking. Then came a number of lean years that brought disaster to the farmers as well as to the business men because of the high cost of living. New Ulm's business men steered clear of the commercial rifts and started a new page in their business history. They adopted the cash system and are no longer chasing the hit and miss customers, that are growing fewer in number from day to day.

On a Saturday evening less than a half century

ago a young married couple knocked at the door of a furniture dealer explaining that they had just been married and in quest of furniture to furnish their modest little home. The furniture dealer was in a great dilemma, not to say predicament, because in an adjoining room two men were waiting for him to join them in a social game of cards. To delay the game might have deprived him of the opportunity to re-enter at a later period. Sizing up the couple a little bit he said: "Well, go inside, look around and if you find what you want call me." The couple entered the establishment while the proprietor disappeared in an adjoining room. After the lapse of a certain time the couple met the proprietor at a side door holding about ten playing cards in his left hand and a glass of beer in his right drinking the beverage and smacking his lips as he talked..

Today a business man pursuing such business methods not only would be pushed to the wall by competitors, but likely would be trampled to death by the crowds that gather on the sidewalks on Saturdays, despite the fact that New Ulm has fewer than 500 inhabitants.

The Pathfinders.

Among the pathfinders who laid the foundation for a permanent settlement either at Industry, New Ulm, Cat Spring or Frelsburg, Fredrich Ernst and Charles Fordtran took the lead and are mentioned by all writers of historial sketches as the vanguard of the German element in Texas. Next in order of rank, prominence, adventure and success at pioneering this section of the state, the names of Scherrer, Bartels. Freis, Pettus, Piper, Amsler, Benninghof, Walter, Wolters, Kleekaemper, Schneider, Biegel, Maerz, Zimmerscheidt, von Roeder, Knolle and Rinn are recorded in the annals of Austin County as well as in the memory of those who made it a part of their life's work to carefully preserve the history of their forbears, as the early homebuilders here prior to the struggle between the states.

Bernard Scherrer

Born in Switzerland Bernard Scherrer directed his footsteps to Texas when a youth, arriving here in the spring of 1832, when Texas was still a Mexican province. On his first visit to Texas he was not favorably impressed with the broad expanse of the territory under Spanish rule, and went to the North in search of a location more adapted to his liking. He went up the Mississippi river as far as Missouri where he met Charles Fordtran, another explorer. Not finding that country to their liking the two of them returned to Texas riding horseback through an unknown wilderness infested with dangerous animals and marauding redskins. The heavy Enfield rifle that Scherrer carried with him on his daring and adventurous rides, both as a means of protection and for bagging game for food, is still in an excellent state of preservation and owned and highly treasured as an heirloom by his grandson, Dr. B. E. Knolle, who himself has long since been advanced to the dignities of Grandfathership.

Scherrer secured a grant of land beyond New Ulm in Colorado County. The grant was not very valuable and not suited for agriculture which prompted Mr. Scherrer to negotiate for a more fertile tract at Biegel settlement, Fayette County, a village named for his friend and compatriot Biegel, who had previously settled there. Mr. Scherrer was an educated man which accounts for his election to the position of alcadee in Fayette County, in the year 1838, by the electors of his district. On another page we reproduce a copy of his commission issued him by Sam Houston, president of the Republic of Texas.

Bartels.

Among the early settlers locating in the Ernst

league, near Industry, were Mr. and Mrs. Bartels. Their matrimonial union being without issue they purchased or adopted a young negro slave who learned to speak their language and respected and obeyed his master and mistress with all filial love and did his part dispelling the monotony and loneliness which often darkened the modest little farm home on the banks of Mill Creek. Bartels, it is said, was an educated man and aside of acquiring several hundred acres of fine fertile farming land adjacent to Mill Creek, managed to accumulate considerable cash money the greater portion of which he lent to his intimate friends who paid him a legitimate rate of interest for the use of it. Bartels preceded his wife in death, however, his slave, Henry Williams, (still living on the farm inherited from his master) and his wife took excellent care of Mrs. Bartels providing her with all comforts of life and brightened her declining days of life. Unfortunately Mrs. Bartels suffered a stroke of paralysis of which she never recovered. For two long years she was an invalid and unable to leave her bed without the assistance given her by her slave and his wife, who bathed, washed, clothed and fed her during her prolonged illness and helplessness, until death relieved her of her pitiful condition.

After both Mr. and Mrs. Bartels had passed away their joint will, providing for the cancellation of all claims due the estate and bequeathing all the residue of their estate, both real and personal, to their slave Henry Williams, was offered for probate.

And that's why old, gray haired Henry Williams is still in possession of a pack of letters written in German three quarters of a century ago and which he treasures highly and keeps, snugly tied to his old deed from Mrs. Bartels.

C. C. Koch

One of the most conspicuous characters of the pioneer days of Industry was C. C. Koch, who settled there about the year 1848. He was married four times. His first wife was the daughter of Mr. and Mrs. Ahlreid who died without issue. For his second wife Koch married Mrs. Ernestine Appel. Of the children born to their matrimonial union only one son, C. T. Koch, one of the oldest business men of New Ulm, survives. The maiden name of Mr. Koch's third wife was Rosalia Machak who died leaving surviving her one daughter, Laura Miller, wife of the late Dr. K. N. Miller of Houston. For his fourth wife Koch married Mrs. Marie Teufel, a sister of the late Oswald Rehm, also a pioneer.

Jack Rinn

Jack (Jacob) Rinn who settled at Post Oak Point near the banks of Pastoren Creek, was among the early settlers who came here at an early date. Mr.

Rinn was instrumental in encouraging immigrants to come to Texas in order that they might eventually become independent citizens. His efforts were crowned with success inasmuch as many cf the new comers made their temporary headquarters with him and got their start in life on his extensive farm. And yet he lived in a modest way avoiding the publicity that was due him because of his hospitality and his willingness to help provide a home for those who followed him to the land of his adoption. He and Mrs. Rinn reared a fine family of boys and girls all of whom followed their parents to the grave save one son, Paul Rinn, who resides at Yoakum, Texas. Scores of grandchildren are proud to trace their lineage to him and to bear his name.

Incomplete List of Early Pioneers who settled at or near New Ulm, Texas, Prior to 1858 and names of their surviving children:

A

Christopher Ashorn, surviving children: W. C. Ashorn, Mrs. Elizabeth Kretzschmar, Edward Ashorn, Sr., Mrs. Chas. Schuette, New Ulm; Mrs. Ignatz Klump, Goliad County.

Otto Aurich. The parents of Otto Aurich settled here at an early date the following grandchildren survive: A. G. Aurich, Oscar Aurich, Paul Aurich, New Ulm. Mrs. Ernst Klump, Rockhouse; Mrs. W. F, Krauss, Round Top: Mrs. Elvira Klatt, Burton; and Aurich of Ledbetter.

B

Charles Bastian, surviving children: Mrs. August Hoppe, Sr., Adolf, August, New Ulm; Mrs. Antonia Bader and Henry Bastian, Star Hill; Charles Bastian, Skidmore; Mrs. Gustav Kretzschmar, Taylor; Mrs. Charles W. Rau, Columbus.

Henry Brune; surviving children: Wm. Brune, Post Oak Point; Mrs. F, Runge and Mrs. Wm. Rinn, New Ulm; Mrs. Henry Rinn, Old Glory.

George Brune; Ed. Brune, Sealy, and Mrs. Elise Koy, New Orleans.

Edward Brune; Grand children survive.

Mr. and Mrs. F. Dorbritz, surviving children: C. A. Dorbritz, New Ulm; Mrs. Louise Albrecht, and Anna Dohmann, Weser; Antonio Deininger, San Antonio;

F

Daniel Find, surviving children: E. C. Find, New Ulm; Mrs. L. J. Rinn, Post Oak Point; Mrs. Emilie Rudloff, Sealy; and Mrs. Auguste Wink, Glidden.

G

Mr. and Mrs. Fritz Gross, surviving children: Louie Gross Post Oak Point; Mrs. John Rinn, New Ulm; Mrs. Wm. Altmann, Nordheim.

H

William Holzmann, surviving children: Mrs. Anna Teufel, Mrs. Reinhold Beckmann, Mrs. E. H. Wangemann, Industry; Mrs. — Witte, Yoakum and Mrs. John Koch, Idaho.

Wm. Hagemann; (Mrs. Hagemann is still living at a serene old age at La Grange) surviving children: Otto, La Grange.

F. Haubold, surviving children: Alvin Haubold, Waco; Mrs. Lena Wotipka, Star Hill; Mrs. Natalia Wink, San Saba, Texas.

Otto Henkhaus: surviving grandchildren.

K

Gottfried Kellner, surviving children: Oscar Kellner and Mrs. J, Weber, New Ulm; G. J. Kellner, Brookshire; Friedrich Kellner, Sealy; Mrs. Schlueter and T. P. Kellner, Houston.

Gottfried Krueger, surviving children: Reinhold, Emil, Albert and Leo, New Ulm; Amandus, Houston; Julius, Oklahoma City; Samuel, San Antonio; Gustav, Brady; Mrs. Henriette Engelking, Waco; and Mrs. Auguste Martens, Nealsville, Wisconsin.

J. C. Krause, surviving children: Franz and Louis Krause, Star Hill; Mrs. August Mueller, Latium.

Nicolaus Kieselbach, surviving child: Mrs. Ottilie Kochendoerfer, Star Hill.

August Klump (Mrs. Klump is still living at the age of 97), surviving children: William and Otto of Stonewall County; Louis of Bellville; Ignatz of Goliad County; Ernst of Rockhouse; Mrs. Emilie Blaschke, Cat Spring; Mrs. Henriette Hines, Greenvine and Albert of Rosebud.

L

George Lingnau, surviving children: George, Needville; August and Mrs. A. W. Becker, New Braunfels; Mrs Paul Dorbritz, Waco; Mrs. Lydia Pagel, Bishop; Mrs. Bertha Mittank, Shiner; Mrs. Mary Mueller, Moulton; Mrs. Elise Baring, Eagle Lake and Louis Lingnau, address unknown.

Karel Lesikar, Mrs. John Stalmach, Nelsonville;

F. F. Lesikar, New Ulm; Mrs. —— Baier, Brenham: J. C. and C. O. Lesikar, Smithville, and Mrs. Anna Schiller, Deanville.

Emil Lesikar; surviving children: Carl Lesikar and Joe Lesikar, New Bremen.

M

Friedrich Miller, surviving children: Mrs. F. H. Kothmann, Mason, Texas; Mrs. W. J. Mogford, Streeter, Texas; Mrs. F. C. Wolters, Schulenburg, Texas; F. B. Miller, Post Oak Point, and A. G. Miller, Beeville, Texas.

Gottlieb Mieth, surviving child, August Mieth, Sealy, Texas.

Kasper Muench, surviving children: Gerhard Muench, New Ulm, and Bernhard Muench, Houston.

Christian Maerz, surviving children: Christian Maerz, Mrs. Emelia Dockal and Mrs. Elise Koneshick, Schoenau; William Maerz, Welcome and Lorenz Maerz Lavaca County.

P

F. A. Peschel, surviving children: A. C. Peschel, New Ulm; Mrs. Chas. Becker, Sr. and August Peschel, Star Hill; Mrs. F. Weige. Industry; Mrs. A Bormann, Wesley, and Max Peschel, Rosebud.

William Persky, surviving children: William Persky, Milam County and Mrs. Meng, Moulton.

Franz Pille, surviving children: Mrs. A. Haubold, Waco; Mrs. William Klump, Stonewall County and Mrs. A. Kellner, Sealy, Texas.

R

Mr. and Mrs. John Rinn, surviving children: Charles, August, Julius, Emil, and Miss Ida Rinn,

New Ulm; Mrs. Adolf Hoppe, Hatchel; Mrs. W. E. Weige, Bellville; Mrs. Hugo Klump, Bartlett; Otto Rinn, Old Glory.

Ludwig Rinn, surviving children: Henry Rinn, Old Glory; H. C. Rinn, Mrs. Richard Galle, Mrs. Otto Heinsohn, Post Oak Point; Mrs. Louis Galle and Mrs. Richard Henniger, Willow Springs; Mrs. H. Veith, Rockhouse; Louis Rinn, Pisek; and Mrs. O. Sonnenberg, Ballinger.

Jacob Rinn, surviving child: Ernst Rinn, Ben Arnold. --- Runge, surviving children: Herman Runge, New Ulm; Willie Runge, Yoakum; Carl Runge, New Braunfels; Mrs. Paul Dittmer, Cat Spring.

S

D. Schweke, surviving children: Ernst and Louis, New Ulm, Mrs. R. F. Glaeser, Post Oak Point and Mrs. Charles Heinsohn. Bartlett.

Lorenz Sailer, surviving children: August W. Sailer, Brenham; Mrs. Bettie Shelburne, Somerville and Mrs. Emma Shelburne, Wallis.

Henry Schuette, surviving children: Mrs. Otto Wienke, New Bremen; Mrs. Anna Ernst, Rule; Mrs. Otto Klump, Old Glory; L. A. Schuette, Alice and Robert Schuette, Brazil, S. A.

— Schiller, surviving child: V. C. Schiller, New Ulm.

V

John Voskamp, surviving children: H. L. Voskamp, New Ulm; Mrs. Henry Trojan, Miss Pauline Voskamp and Henry Voskamp, Weimar.

W

Adam Wangemann, surviving children: Mrs.

Henriette Becker and Mrs. Hugo Becker, Brenham; Mrs. F. B. Miller, Post Oak Point; Arthur Wangemann, Corpus Christi, Texas.

Ernst Wangemann, surviving children: E. H. Wangemann, Industry; Mrs. Louise Meyer and Mrs. Almietha Walcak, San Antonio, Texas.

Thomas Wangler, surviving children: August Wangler, New Ulm; Mrs. Fritz Hattermann, Fayetteville, Texas.

Wolters, surviving children: Max Wolters, Shiner; Robert Wolters, Schulenburg, Texas.

P. Witte, surviving child: Mrs. Joe Holzmann, New Ulm.

C. A. Weige, surviving children: Adolf, Mrs. Minna Peschel, and Mrs. Emma Altmann, New Ulm; Mrs. Sophie Luedecke, Hallettsville, and Herm. Weige, Bartlett, Texas.

Wm. Voelkel, surviving children: Mrs. Herman Schroeder and Mrs. Emil Rinn, Industry.

Z

Heinrich Zulauf, surviving children: Mrs. Anna Sternenberg and Miss C. Zulauf, Star Hill.

The whereabouts of the following named pioneer families or their posterity is not known: Colonel Henderson, Georgie, Muckleroy, Sullivan, Waddel, Helweg Daniels, Schoelman, Krell, See, Baur. Bauer, Sitter, Hinze, Tafel, Roedel, Fahrenholdt, Wagner, Lueschner, Wisehnevski, Heinemann, Haemerlein, and scores of others.

Industry

B

Fredrich Boelsche, surviving children: W. F., H. H. and Mrs. Herman Lahrmann, Industry; Mrs. C. T. Koch, New Ulm, and Mrs. Lina Eckermann, Houston.

Henry Breihan, surviving children: August and William Breihan, Rt. 1, New Ulm, Texas.

Andreas Buenger, surviving children: Adolf Buenger, Mrs. R. D. Franke and Miss Emilie Buenger, Industry.

Albert Beckmann, surviving children: Robert and Reinhold, Industry; Mrs. F. A. Weige, New Ulm; Dr. Paul Beckmann, La Grange; Dr. Willie Beckmann, Missouri; Mrs. Franke, El Campo, and Miss Alma Beckmann, Temple.

D

Theodor Daum, surviving children: Herman and Miss Auguste Daum, Industry; Mrs. Robert Berndt, Perry, Falls County.

E

August Eckermann, surviving children: Mrs. Herman Dudensing, Post Oak Point; Mrs. Theodor Fertsch, Halletsville; Mrs. R. Henniger, Ballinger and Herman Eckermann, Houston.

Henry Eckermann; F. H. Eckermann and Mrs. Wm. Neumann, Rockhouse; Otto Eckermann, Holland.

Ernst Eckermann: Rudolf, Welcome; Edmund and Alex and Mrs. Theo Koch, Industry; Ernst of Greenvine and Mrs. August Gramms, Cost,

Texas.

Louis Eckermann (Mrs. Eckermann is still living at the age of 90). Surviving children: Mrs. Henry Luetge, Sr.; Mrs. Fritz Hupe; Mrs. Otto Lindemann, Industry; Edwin, Fayetteville, Rt. 4; Adolf, San Antonio; Louis and Mrs. ---, Miles, Texas.

Fredrich Ernst, surviving grand children: Herman, Ferdinand, August, Fredrich and Mrs. Ed. Schroeder, Industry; Adolf, Alice, and Mrs. Herman Buenger, Ellinger.

F

Charles Fordtran, surviving children: R. L. Fordtran, Industry; Tom Fordtran, Fayetteville.

Charles Franke, surviving children: Ernst and Miss Bertha Franke, Industry; Mrs. H. W. Huebner, Welcome; Mrs. A. A. Laake, Cuero; Mrs. Agnes Ringener, Bellville; Mrs. A. F. Wotipka, Smithville; Mrs. John Light, La Grange; Mrs. Alex Eckermann, Schoenau; Oscar Franke, Mexico and Max, New Ulm. Mrs. Franke is still living.

Rudolf Franke, surviving children: R. D. Franke and Eddy Franke, Industry; Mrs. W. O. Schramm, Glenflora.

Friedrich Fisches, surviving children: Mrs. Edward Lindemann and Willie Fisches, Industry; Mrs. Willie Moeller, Bartlett.

G

Christian Gollmer; no surviving children.

Hugo Gloss, surviving children: Gustav and Henry Gloss, Runnels County; Mrs. Max Ernst, Mrs. Henry Ernst and Mrs. Willie Ruppert, address unknown.

H

Henry Haverlah, surviving grandchildren.

K

---- Kliem, surviving children: W. C. Kliem and Mrs. Otto Kohlloeffel, Sealy.

Ernst Knolle, surviving children: E. M. Knolle, New Ulm.

William Knolle, surviving children: Dr. W. L. F. Knolle, Washington, Texas; A. L. Knolle, and Mrs. A. L. Baring, Houston; Mrs. A. W. Brill, Austin and Chas F. Knolle, Industry, Texas.

Herman Knolle, surviving children: Dr. B, E. Knolle, Industry and Dr. A. P. Knolle, Ellinger, Texas.

John Kroulik, surviving children: Mrs. J. J. Frnka, New Ulm; Dr. John Kroulik, Nelsonville; Dr. Frank Kroulik, Joe Kroulik and William Kroulik, Smithville, and Rudolf Kroulik, Shiner.

L

August Lindemann: Edward Lindemann and Mrs. Henry Raeke, Industry; August Lindemann, Willie Lindemann, Mrs. August Raeke and Willibald Lindemann, Gonzales; and Otto Lindemann, Rockhouse.

M

Max Meissner, surviving children: Mrs. Robert Beckmann and Mrs. C. O. Sternenberg, Industry; Mrs. Julius Steck, California; Miss Ella Meissner, Bellville; George Meissner, Ft. Worth and Oscar Meissner.

Andreas Muenzler, surviving children: L. C., Willow Spring; Mrs. Sophie Breihan, Bartlett; G. G. Muenzler, Avoca, Texas; Mrs. Rosina Walter, Amarillo, Texas.

N

Fritz Niebuhr, surviving children: F. H. and L. A. Niebuhr, Industry.

Henry Neumann: H. A. Neumann, Robert Neumann and Ben Neumann, Houston.

R

Christian Rudloff, surviving children: Otto, Bellville; Mrs. Bertha Dorbritz, New Ulm; Albert, Industry; and Mrs. Augusta Schlabach, Goliad County.

Henry Raeke, surviving children: Henry Raeke, Rockhouse; Carl Raeke, Bartlett; August Raeke, Gonzales and Willie Raeke, Rockhouse.

S

Franz Schramm, surviving children: H. A. Schramm, Industry; Joe and Robert Schramm, Brenham; Dr. Chas. Schramm, Fayetteville; William Schramm El Campo; August and Hugo Schramm, New York; Mrs. Chas. Find, El Campo; Mrs. Walters, San Antonio.

Carl Schulze (Mrs. Schulze is still living at a serene old age), surviving children: C. A. Schulze, and Mrs. Adolf Buenger, Industry; O. L. Schulze, Houston.

Fritz Schroeder, surviving children; Herman, Otto and Eddy, Industry.

F. W. Sternenberg, grandchildren survive.

Fredrich Schmidt, surviving children: Mrs. E. C. Find, New Ulm; Otto Schmidt, Austin; August Schmidt, and Mrs. Ella Neumann, Yoakum.

Max Schmidt, surviving children: Mrs. George Koch, Temple; Mrs. E. H. Sternenberg, Norheim; and Mrs. ---, El Campo.

W

Jacob, Wuertz, surviving child: Mrs. C. H. Berndt, Industry.

Ernst Witte; surviving children: Mrs. B. E. Knolle, Industry; Mrs. Arthur Warnasch, Shelby; Mrs. O. G. Pophanken, Eagle Lake; Dr. Wallie Witte, Waco; Dr. Kenney Witte, New Orleans, and Mrs. Hodde Brenham.

Frelsburg

Louis Brune, surviving children: Florenz Brune, Frelsburg; Herman Brune, Columbus; Mrs. Paul Machemchl and Mrs. Ernst Laas, Bellville.

Henry Bruedigam, surviving children: Fred Bruedigam, Mrs. Sophie Brune, Mrs. Frederika Warschak and Mrs. Ed. Venghaus, Frelsburg.

Theodor Becker, surviving children: August Becker, Frelsburg; Willie Becker, Bellville; Mrs. Louis Pflughaupt, Post Oak Point; Mrs. Mary Schmidt, Welcome.

Fred Kollmann surviving children: F. G. Kollmann, Frelsburg; Louis Kollmann, ----; Edwin A. Kollmann, Kennedy; Mrs. H. A. Buescher, Columbus; Mrs. L. H. Baron, Bellville; Mrs. Dr. H. E. Mitshel, Shiner; Mrs. Wangemann, Mrs. Moeckel and Miss Ophilea Kollmann, San Antonio.

D. Pophanken, surviving children: R. E. Pophanken, New Ulm; T. A. Pophanken, Post Oak Point; O. G. and Willie Pophanken, Eagle Lake.

John Moeckel, surviving child: Emil Moeckel, Frelsburg.

In The Name and by the Authority of The Republic of Texas.

To All To Whom These Presents Shall Come Or May Concern:— Greeting:

Be it known, THAT I, SAM HOUSTON. THE PRESIDENT OF THE REPUBLIC OF TEXAS, reposing special trust and full confidence in the honor, patriotism, fidelity, skill and capacity of Bernard Scherrer do, by the power vested in me by law, hereby COMMISSION him, the said BERNARD SCHERRER to the office of JUSTICE OF THE PEACE, in the third captain's district, in the county of Fayette—He having been elected to said office by the qualified electors of said district, giving and hereby granting to him, the said Bernard Sherrer—full power and authority as such, to exercise and discharge all and singular duties, obligations and trusts to his said office in any wise appertaining, by the constitution and laws of this republic.

To have and to hold the same and all and every the honors, fees, perquisities and dues thereunto belonging, for and during and until the full end and term of two years from the day of his election.

Given under my hand and the seal of my office, at Houston this Twenty-sixth day of January, A.D. 1838, and of the Independence of said Republic the Second.

R. A. Irion
Sec. of State   Sam Houston

More Books about Texas

from Texianer Verlag

A Lone Star Arises in Texas

Texas is well known to everyone as the setting for Indian tales and Wild West romances and most have also heard of the oil wells and sulfur pits, cattle herds, and cotton fields that secure it a place in the world economy. But who knows anything about the fact that in the vast areas that stretch between the Mississippi and the Rio Grande deep into the Plains, historical events as charming as they are significant to have taken place, that Texas also has a place in world history? And yet it does! Texas has by no means led an insular existence far removed from the course of great events, but has stood in the midst of the force field of the manifold political tensions which determined the development of the North American continent. Against the backdrop of its wildernesses and prairies, an eventful, colorful and turbulent historical spectacle unfolded, telling of the doings and activities of many men and nations, of a world full of wild, harsh sounds, shrouded in the air of an adventurous romanticism known only to the colonial and frontier era of North America. The curses of Spanish soldiers and the prayers of Spanish monks are mixed with the voices of French rangers and the war cries of Indian horsemen until all these sounds are drowned out by the ax-blow of Anglo-Saxon pioneers who penetrate the fertile plains and valleys of the country with the strength of rolled-up shirt-sleeves.

A Boy's Civil War Story

From the original fly leaf: "A distinguished American statesman and member of the bar, known chiefly heretofore as the Secretary of Commerce and Labor in the Cabinet of President Taft, as director in important enterprises, and as counsel for various corporations and individuals, here makes his bow as author (at the fine age of nearly 88) of a good book giving his recollections of life as it was lived, and war as it was waged, in the days of 1861 to 1865 during the conflict between the States.

A penetrating pen-picture of things and places that few persons living today have experienced for themselves, and that still fewer are now capable of recollecting, Mr. Nagel's book also takes the happy reader to the Germany of student days, where as a young man the author entered the University of Berlin, which later was to confer on him the honorary degree as Doctor of Political Science. Known not less for his good works than for his great accomplishments, the present modest memoir will afford the reader both information and pleasure, and put in permanent form a record of days and ways that will not come again." This edition has been augmented with copious footnotes and illustrations in order to assist the modern reader better understand the context of the times.

The Millheim and Cat Spring Pioneers
German Immigrants Building a New Life in Texas

This book is a continuation of an effort began in 2015 by a handful of individuals with an interest in the history of the German settlements at Cat Spring and Millheim in Austin County, Texas. Three of the early literary works by Millheim settlers have been republished — Experiences and Observations and A History of Austin County by William Andreas Trenckmann, and A Boy's Civil War Story by Charles Nagel. Obscure books, newspaper and periodical articles, literary novels and plays written about the area by former residents a century or so ago have been identified.

An inventory of all such documents and their current status as to public availability has been developed. This book presents a brief history of the extended Cat Spring–Millheim community in western Austin County, along with reproductions of several articles written by early area pioneers such as Robert Kleberg, Rosa von Roeder Kleberg, Caroline Ernst von Hineuber, Adalbert Regenbrecht and Ottilie Fuchs Goeth. We provide brief biographies of many of the early settlers including Elemenech Swearingen, Ludwig von Roeder, Robert Kleberg, Carl Amsler, Friedrich Engelking, Andreas Trenckmann, Robert Kloss, Gustav Maetze, Dr. Herman Nagel, Adalbert Regenbrecht, Rev. Arnost Bergmann and Louis Constant. Also summarized are the significant literary works created by early settlers in the area, including William Andreas Trenckmann, Charles Nagel, Johannes Christlieb Nathanael Romberg and Adolph Fuchs. Several of these long out-of-print works are reproduced herein.

A German Paradise in Texas

The Fate of German Emigrants to Texas in the 1840's

A gripping historical novel about the Germans who left their home country more than 150 years ago. False promises of a better life and incompetent organisers attracted thousands who had little to lose back home to look for a new life in Texas with the hope of creating a New Germany free from tyranny and poverty. These courageous people created much of the culture of Texas today. This emotive rendering of Scheffel's monumental 'lost' heart-rending classic makes this story available for English language readers for the first time. Notes are provided for additional background information.

Texas 1840

Origin and Current State of the New, Independent State of Texas: A Contribution to the History / Statistics and Geography of this Century Collected in the Country Itself

Anyone who is as fascinated about the era surrounding the establishment of the Republic of Texas as I am, will understand my excitement on discovering this book in German written in 1840. G.A. Scherpf was a German who had been living for some time in New York and decided to undertake an expedition to see with his own eyes which of the conflicting reports about Texas were true. He became so enamored with the country that he decided to settle there himself. As an economist and a highly educated person, he has taken painstaking trouble to collect all the data which would be relevant to anyone considering emigration from Germany.

This was a time when conditions in Prussia and Germany as a whole were anything less than comfortable. It was marked with wars and deprivation. Many, especially of the lower working classes, were living under oppressive domination in what was still basically a feudal system, with no hope of bettering themselves. At that time, land was the number one priority if one wanted to gain some independence and a minimum of prosperity. The chances of attaining that were just about zero as most land was in the hands of an inflexible and self-sufficing aristocracy. A bureaucratic state and a military culture were further hindrances to any kind of progress. The offer of land up for grabs, even in a far away country, was extremely tempting and if one could raise the capital for the arduous sea journey, possibly the only alternative to a miserable life on the edge of starvation. So the stories of the opportunities of Texas abounded and many wrote pamphlets and books, often colored and biased to encourage emigration. Scherpf tries to bring clarity amongst all of this and claims to paint an unbiased picture. However, he had obviously fallen completely in love with Texas and his bias often shines through his attempted objectivity at times. He also obviously strictly abhors the use of alcoholic drinks (liquor) and uses every opportunity to convince the reader of the necessity for abstinence. It certainly did play a negative role among the early colonists and it is understandable that he would want to warn his readers of the dangers of its abuse. As well as a detailed description of the country's historical, political and economic situation, he offers detailed records of the climate at the time. Here, the potential emigrant of 1840 would have had a handbook at his fingertips which would give him all the necessary information to make the life-changing decision of going to Texas. Thus it provides today's reader with a fascinating insight into the world of the Republic of Texas in 1840. Readers of German in today's Texas have become rare and emigration to Texas for Germans is no longer an issue. It is for that reason that I decided to translate this enormously important work into English to give the opportunity of sharing this discovery to those who would like to better understand the world of their ancestors.

The Story of My Life

Written for my Children Summer 1939

Caroline Mackensen married Julius Romberg who was the youngest son of the famous Texas-German poet Johannes Romberg. She tells a colorful story from her early life starting in Shelby in 1856 and describes in detail how life developed and the challenges which had to be overcome in this period in Texas. It is a piece of valuable historic documentation made available here for an interested public.

Reminiscences of Louise Romberg Fuchs 1927

Translated from the German by Helen and Gertrude Franke 1936

We, who live in the Machine Age, can scarcely imagine how our grandparents and parents, who came from a populous country, the home of their parents, and moved with them to the thinly settled state of Texas, passed their youth—under circumstances and surroundings so entirely different from those under which we grandchildren and children live. Therefore, we gladly listen when Grandmother or Grandfather tells of that time: the pioneer days with their sorrows and joys! And so the children and grandchildren of Louise Fuchs have asked her to write down her Reminiscences, so that those days will not vanish for us in the stream of time.

Letters from America 1833-1838

Wilhelm Hübsch's Letters from America offers a fascinating and detailed view into the life and struggles on the American frontier. Hübsch emigrated to America in 1833 on the Olbers, a 152-foot-long sailing ship, as a member of the Mainzer Emigration Society. His decision to venture to the new world was founded upon a sense of adventure, compelled by political circumstances and encouragement of glowing reports of a better life in America. His letters begin with a description of the 55-day trip that took members of the society to New Orleans, and up the Mississippi and Arkansas Rivers to Little Rock. There the settlers faced illness and hardship, compounded by unhealthy air and bad weather.

Struggling to establish themselves, a full third of the company ended up in the grave within three years. Survivors who were able departed. Like most of them, Wilhelm was unable to sell his possessions when he left America. Wilhelm's enthusiasm evaporated as his health and resources were depleted. Enfeebled and disheartened, Wilhelm ultimately resolved to regain what he had left behind, a loving supportive family and the pursuit of a career.

History of Austin County, Texas
Edited and published in 1899 as a supplement to the Bellville Wochenblatt

In the spring of 1933, exactions of old age forced William Trenckmann to sell his newspaper to the National Weeklies of Minnesota but he remained its editor in all matters pertaining to Texas. Mr. Trenckmann was regarded as one of the best informed men in Texas on state and national affairs and during his many years in the newspaper business wrote considerably about the history of the state and the nation while in the making. From the date of the founding of his newspaper, he wrote each week a summary of national and state news for the readers of his weekly newspaper.

Politically, Mr. Trenckmann was a democrat, not in the partisan interpretation of the word but rather in the light of the tenets of justice, tolerance, freedom of speech and freedom of press, to which ideals he remained loyal throughout life, with a loyalty stimulated by the teachings of his father, a disciple of Kant, who was born in Germany in the time when the teachings of that philosopher on the concept of duty were beginning to spread.

The Engelking Letters

A Collection of Letters Written by or Pertaining to Ferdinand Friedrich Engelking 1810-1885

The Engelking Letters is a collection of letters written by or pertaining to Ferdinand Friedrich Engelking 1810-1885 and translated and annotated by Flora von Roeder. They tell their own story of the struggles of this early Texas pioneer who, despite many hardships, gradually established himself and his family in the new Republic of Texas after emigrating from Germany. Sometimes the reader will be reduced to tears when reading of the death of dear ones and infants. Despite all the set backs, Ferdinand's robust pioneering character and the support of his beloved wife enabled the couple to sustain themselves and become a meeting point of hospitality for early settlers. Together with the teacher Maetze, they were able to found Texas' first German High School.

These Are the Generations (2 Volumes)

A Biography of the von Roeder Family and its Role in Texas History

Flora von Roeder is one of thousands of direct descendants of a family in a Germanic entity in Europe called Anhalt. The family can theoretically be traced back to 1218 and is documented back to 1390. Those are spans of 795 and 613 years, respectively. Her intent here is to show how the main branch of this family emigrated from the European continent to the North American continent and to show its ability to establish roots and grow and multiply in an entirely different lifestyle under primitive circumstances into a clan that stretches today into many U.S. States, Canada, Mexico, back into European France and Germany, and to Hong Kong, and Australia.

Between 1834 and today, there are as many as eight or nine generations of this family, most of whom were born in the U.S. Many do not carry the original surname, and many who do have changed it. Because the English alphabet does not carry the umlaut, an "e" was inserted after the "o" to make the spelling more accurate, and that made the pronunciation more confusing. Today we have "von Roeders," "von Raders," "von Raeders", and many have just dropped the "von" altogether, so we have just "Roeders." And, of course, there were the name changes through marriage; i.e., Engelking, Kleberg, Eckhardt, Binz, Wundt, Flato, Van Hutton, Regenbrecht, etc. Nevertheless, all can still be traced back to those knights called Koppen (Jacob) and Hans Röder or von Röder in a feudal letter awarding them noble lands at Harzgerode, Anhalt, in 1390.

Please visit us at www.texianer.com

www.ingramcontent.com/pod-product-compliance
Lightning Source LLC
LaVergne TN
LVHW032005070526
838202LV00058B/6304